15·MINUTE
COVER LETTER

write an effective cover letter right now

MICHAEL FARR

with

LOUISE M. KURSMARK

JIST
Works
America's Career Publisher

PART OF JIST'S HELP IN A HURRY™ SERIES

15-MINUTE COVER LETTER

© 2005 by Michael Farr and Louise M. Kursmark

Published by JIST Works, an imprint of JIST Publishing, Inc.
8902 Otis Avenue
Indianapolis, IN 46216-1033
Phone: 1-800-648-JIST   Fax: 1-800-JIST-FAX   E-mail: info@jist.com

Visit our Web site at **www.jist.com** for information on JIST, free job search tips, book chapters, and ordering instructions for our many products! For free information on 14,000 job titles, visit **www.careeroink.com**.

Quantity discounts are available for JIST books. Please call our Sales Department at 1-800-648-5478 for a free catalog and more information.

Acquisitions and Development Editor: Lori Cates Hand
Interior Designer: Aleata Howard
Page Layout: Troy Barnes
Cover Designer: Katy Bodenmiller
Proofreader: Linda Quigley
Indexer: Kelly D. Henthorne
Printed in the United States of America
10 09 08 07 06 05   9 8 7 6 5 4 3 2

Library of Congress Cataloging-in-Publication Data

Farr, J. Michael
15-minute cover letter : write an effective cover letter right now /
Michael Farr with Louise M. Kursmark.
      p. cm.
Includes bibliographical references and index.
ISBN 1-59357-175-5 (alk. paper)
1. Cover letters. 2. Résumés (Employment) 3. Job hunting. I. Title:
Fifteen-minute cover letter. II. Kursmark, Louise. III. Title.
HF5383.F315 2005
650.14'2--dc22   2005005196

We have been careful to provide accurate information in this book, but it is possible that errors and omissions have been introduced. Please consider this in making any career plans or other important decisions. Trust your own judgment above all else and in all things.

Trademarks: All brand names and product names used in this book are trade names, service marks, trademarks, or registered trademarks of their respective owners.

ISBN 1-59357-175-5

About This Book

This book will teach you how to write personalized, effective cover letters very quickly. We don't want you to get frustrated and bogged down in the process, but neither do we want you to dash off something that is quick but not effective. We give you techniques to help you move rapidly through the opening, middle, and closing sections of your cover letters; we tell you when mail or e-mail is most appropriate; and we tell you what you should do *before* you write your cover letters to make them truly effective. And we provide lots of sample cover letters to review for ideas to use in your own.

Cover letters are just one important part of the job search, so we also provide information on thank-you letters, e-mail, and other job search correspondence that, when used effectively, can make your transition to a new job smoother and faster. A short but powerful chapter on how you can improve your resume in just 15 minutes is also included, and we close out with a key chapter on job search —what works, what doesn't, and how you can manage an effective search in just seven steps.

After all, changing jobs and changing careers is no longer a rare event. Many workers choose to or are forced to look for work every few years. So learning methods that work, and work quickly, will help you the rest of your working life.

Contents

Chapter 5: Improve Your Resume in 15 Minutes 110

Chapter 6: Seven Steps to Getting a Good Job in Less Time 139

A Brief Introduction to Using This Book

You are all ready to start your job search—or so you think. You have written a great resume, turned up some promising leads, and now need to send your resume with a cover letter to various people in advance of an interview.

But for too many job seekers, the job search comes to a screeching halt at this point. Questions like these come to mind:

- What should I say in my cover letter?
- Can I write one letter and use it for every situation?
- How much background information should I provide?
- What do they really want to know?
- Do I have to match up perfectly for every requirement in the job posting?
- Should I quickly summarize all of my positions?
- Do I have to share information about why I left my last job?
- Do they care about why I'm looking?
- How can I quickly get the attention of busy hiring managers?
- Should I mail or e-mail my cover letter and resume?

It's no wonder that the task of quickly sending out resumes can become a time-consuming, difficult challenge and a real roadblock to a swift, successful search.

With *15-Minute Cover Letter*, we want to change all that. We give you strategies, ideas, and examples that will make the process of producing your cover letters quick, easy, and foolproof. Using these guidelines, you won't become bogged down in the task of writing and sending an effective cover letter, and you can keep your job search moving ahead.

Because our theme is "quick," we haven't loaded down the book with hundreds of examples. Instead, we have given you dozens of *good* examples that illustrate our key points. These include

- 50 complete cover letters and thank-you letters
- Additional samples of language for the opening, middle, and closing sections of your cover letters
- Worksheets to help you organize and keep track of material for your cover letters
- Examples of quick notes, JIST Cards (a mini-resume), and job proposals
- 12 professionally written sample resumes that illustrate our key points for improving your resume

If you are like most job seekers, you will go immediately to the section of the book that deals with your most pressing need—whether that is how to get a cover letter out the door in the next 15 minutes, how to quickly improve your resume, or how to manage your job search for the fastest, best results. But we hope you will take the time to skim through all the sections of the book. All components of your job search—your cover letters, resume, follow-up correspondence, search strategy, network contacts, interview responses, and more—are interrelated, so the more proficient and knowledgeable you become in the entire process, the more successful you'll be. You can't accomplish a job search in 15 minutes, but you can accomplish a lot in each 15-minute segment you allot to it—beginning with the 15-minute cover letter.

We wish you well.

P.S.: Writing this book was a team effort. Mike Farr provided much of the job search and "how-to" text, and Louise Kursmark provided much additional text and created the sample letters and resumes throughout the book. Our editor, Lori Cates Hand, provided essential help with the concept, coordination, and development of the book; Aleata Howard did the interior design; and other JIST staff handled a variety of other tasks well. Thanks!

Chapter 1

Quick Tips for Writing a Cover Letter in 15 Minutes

Cover letters are an essential component of your job search. During your search and transition, you will write many different letters or e-mails to "cover" your resume. In essence, cover letters tell your readers why you are contacting them. Often they are your very first opportunity to make an impression on a hiring decision-maker. They offer you the golden opportunity to link your unique set of skills, experiences, talents, and interests with a particular company or job opportunity. They are your formal introduction to people who can be extremely influential in your job search, and they prepare your reader for all of the details, experiences, and accomplishments you have highlighted in your resume.

In our experience working with all levels of job seekers in hundreds of professions, we have found that writing cover letters is perhaps the greatest stumbling block to an efficient job search. The resume has been written, polished, and is ready to go. Now faced with writing an individual cover letter each time they want to send out a resume, job seekers struggle to find the right words and tone. They worry about not including enough information or the right information. They debate whether they need to point out a match for every qualification listed in a job posting. And they tell us they spend far too much time in all of this struggle, worry, and debate— time that they could better spend expanding their network or following up on leads or preparing for interviews.

We understand the problem, and in this book we provide a solution— a simple, foolproof formula so that you can quickly write letters that convey the right message in the right tone to the many people you'll be contacting during your career transition.

Cover Letters: Why You Need Them and How to Use Them

It is not appropriate to send a resume to someone without explaining why. Whether you're mailing, faxing, or e-mailing your resume, it is important to provide a letter along with your resume—a cover letter (or cover message, in the case of e-mailing). Even when you post your resume in an online database (also known as a resume bank), the Web site where you're posting often has a place where you can upload or paste a cover letter. A cover letter highlights your key qualifications, explains your situation, and asks the recipient for some specific action, consideration, or response.

Because each circumstance is different, you can't write just one cover letter and expect that it will be appropriate in every situation. But remember, our focus in this book is helping you to move quickly through the process of creating your cover letters. By breaking these letters down to their essentials, we give you a framework and a process that will work for *most* situations, along with dozens of examples that will give you ideas and inspiration for both common situations and unusual circumstances.

Only Two Groups of People Will Receive Your Cover Letters

If you think about it, you will send a resume and cover letter to only two groups of people:

- People you know.
- People you don't know.

We realize this sounds overly simple, but it's true. And this observation makes it easier to understand how you might structure your letters to each group. Before we explain our "formula" and show you some useful and effective cover letter samples for both groups, let's first review some basics regarding writing cover letters in general.

> **Note:** *While many situations require writing a formal letter, a simple note will do in many instances. Additional information on informal notes is in chapter 4.*

Seven Quick Tips for Writing a Superior Cover Letter

No matter who you are writing to, virtually every good cover letter should follow these guidelines.

1. Write to Someone in Particular

Avoid sending a cover letter "To whom it may concern" or using some other impersonal opening. We all get enough junk mail, and if you don't send your letter to someone by name, it will be treated like junk mail.

2. Make Absolutely No Errors

One way to offend people right away is to misspell their names or use incorrect titles. If you are not 100 percent certain, call and verify the correct spelling of the name and other details before you send the letter. Also, review your letters carefully to be sure that they contain no typographical, grammatical, or other errors.

3. Personalize Your Content

We've never been impressed by form letters, and you should not use them. Those computer-generated letters that automatically insert a name (known as merge mailings) never fool anyone, and we find cover letters done in this way offensive. It's likely your recipients will think so, too. While some resume and cover letter books recommend that you send out lots of these "broadcast letters" to people you don't know, you will most likely find that doing so wastes time and money. Small, targeted mailings to a carefully selected group of prospective employers can be effective if you tailor your cover letter to each recipient, but large mass mailings are a waste of time. If you can't customize your letter in some way, don't send it.

But that doesn't mean you can't use *some* of the material in one cover letter for other letters as well. In fact, this is one of our top tips to make writing your letters easier and more efficient. In chapter 2 we show you how to do this and how to incorporate some repeatable material into your customized letters.

4. Present a Good Appearance

Your contacts with prospective employers should always be professional, so buy good-quality stationery and matching envelopes for times when you'll be mailing or hand-delivering a letter and resume. For your cover letters, use papers and envelopes that match or complement your resume paper. The standard 8 1/2 × 11 paper size is typically used, but you can also use the smaller Monarch-size paper with matching envelopes. For colors, we recommend white, ivory, or light beige—whatever matches your resume paper. Cover letters are almost never handwritten anymore; employers expect them to be word processed and produced with excellent print quality.

Use a standard letter format that complements your resume type and format. You might find it easier to use your word-processing software's template or "wizard" functions than to create a format from scratch. Your letters don't have to be fancy; they do have to look professional. And don't forget the envelope! It should be typed and printed carefully, without errors.

> **Tip:** Undoubtedly, you will send many of your cover letters as e-mail messages. All of the rules we discuss for traditional cover letters apply equally to e-mail cover letters. Just because e-mail is a less formal means of communicating, don't be careless with writing, spelling, grammar, punctuation, or presentation. We do recommend that your e-mail cover letters be a bit shorter and crisper than your traditional paper letters. You need to capture attention before the reader hits "delete"! Several of the sample cover letters in chapter 3 are presented in e-mail format, without headings or stationery, to give you some examples of how to present these letters for best results.

5. Begin with a Friendly Opening

Start your letter with a reminder of any prior contacts and the reason for your correspondence now. The examples throughout this book will give you some ideas on how to handle this.

6. Target Your Skills and Experiences

To do this well, you must know something about the organization, the job opportunity, or the person with whom you are dealing. Present any relevant background that may be of particular interest to the person to whom you are writing.

7. Close with an Action Statement

Don't close your letter without clearly identifying what you will do next. We do not recommend that you leave it up to the employer to contact you because that doesn't guarantee a response. Close on a positive note and let the employer know how and when you will be following up.

Writing Cover Letters to People You Know

It is always best if you know the person to whom you are writing. Any written correspondence—no matter how powerful!—is less effective than personal contact, so the ideal circumstance is to send a resume and cover letter after having spoken with the person directly.

> **Tip:** *Using a few simple techniques, it is possible to make the acquaintance of all sorts of people. That's why we say that it wastes time and money to send your resume or cover letter to strangers—it is relatively easy to make direct contact. Chapter 6 provides details on how to make contact with people you don't know, and we recommend that you learn more about this.*

For example, it is far more effective to first call someone who has advertised in the paper than to simply send a letter and resume. You can come to know people through the Yellow Pages, personal referrals, and other ways. You might not have known them yesterday, but you can get to know them today.

So, for the purposes of teaching you good job search principles, we'll assume you have made some sort of personal contact before sending your resume. Within this assumption are hundreds of variations, but we will review the most common situations and let you adapt them to your own circumstances.

The Four Types of Cover Letters to People You Know

You will have one of four basic situations when sending cover letters to people you know. Each situation requires a different approach. The situations are presented below, along with an explanation. We'll provide sample cover letters for each situation later.

The four types of cover letters illustrate an approach that can be used in getting interviews, which is the real task in the job search. Look at the samples for each type of cover letter and see how, in most cases, it assumes that personal contact has been made before the resume was sent.

1. **An interview is scheduled, and a specific job opening may interest you.** In this case, you have already arranged an interview for a job opening that interests you, and the cover letter should provide details of your experience that relate to the specific job.

2. **An interview is scheduled, but no specific job is available.** In chapter 6, we explain in more detail why this situation is such a good one for you to set up. In essence, this is a letter you will send for an exploratory interview with an employer who does not have a specific opening for you now but who might in the future. This is fertile ground for finding job leads where no one else may be looking.

3. **An interview has already taken place.** Many people overlook the importance of sending a letter after an interview. This is a time to say that you want the job (if that is the case, your letter should say so) and to add any details on why you think you can do the job well.

4. **No interview is scheduled—yet.** There are situations where you just can't arrange an interview before you send a resume and cover letter. For example, you may be trying to see a person, but that person is on vacation. In these cases, sending a good cover letter and resume will make any later contacts more effective.

Sample Cover Letters to People You Know

The following are sample cover letters for the four preceding situations. Note that they use different formats and styles to show you the range of styles that are appropriate. Each addresses a different situation, and each incorporates all of the cover letter–writing guidelines presented earlier in this chapter.

Keep in mind that the best cover letter is one that follows your having set up an interview. Anything else is just second best, at best.

Sample Cover Letter 1: Pre-Interview, for a Specific Job Opening (Sarah Rubin)

Comments: This writer called first and arranged an interview, the best possible approach. Note how she briefly summarizes her strongest qualifications for this specific job opening. To convey some of the intangibles that can make a real difference when choosing among several comparable candidates, she includes a brief recommendation from an executive at her current company, praising her for her persistence and professionalism.

SARAH T. RUBIN

7314 74th Ave NE   206-849-3456 (Home)
Seattle, WA 98130   s_rubin@earthlink.net   206-300-2379 (Mobile)

April 30, 2005

Mr. Mark Anders
Northwest Financial Advisors
2150 Commercial Parkway, Suite 4-B
Seattle, WA 98249

Dear Mr. Anders:

Thank you for speaking with me this morning about your current opening for a Compliance Specialist. As you suggested, I am sending along my resume to give you additional information prior to our meeting next week. It expands on these qualifications that are essential for success as a Compliance Specialist:

- Nine years of experience in banking and financial services, including participation in audit procedures and in-depth involvement with the full range of compliance issues.
- History of initiative and leadership in identifying and reducing compliance risks.
- Strong skills in tracking, monitoring, documenting, and reporting.
- Ability to manage multiple detailed projects simultaneously.

My position at Standard Financial has been eliminated due to a downsizing. As evidence of the value of my work there, the compliance role will be assumed by the company's chief operating officer, who has commended me for my professionalism and "get the job done" attitude.

I look forward to our meeting at 10:30 on Wednesday and learning more about this exciting opportunity with your company.

Sincerely,

Sarah T. Rubin

enclosure: resume

Sample Cover Letter 2: Pre-Interview, No Specific Job Opening (Darryl Poston)

Comments: This letter illustrates how the writer has built upon a casual in-person meeting to initiate a formal discussion about future career options. Although no job opening exists, he is wise in assuming that there will be one in the future. He is planting the seeds to be first in line when an opening does occur. Not only that, he is strengthening his professional network and making himself more visible and memorable within the new industry he is trying to penetrate.

DARRYL T. POSTON

4525 Carmel Court, Indianapolis, IN 46210
317-204-8040 ▪ darrylposton@aol.com

April 30, 2005

Sharon Hanrahan, Sales Manager
Alpha Omega Services
252 Court Street
Indianapolis, IN 46201

Dear Sharon:

I am looking forward to meeting with you on Friday to continue the conversation we started at last month's Downtowners event. We agreed that one of the characteristics of a successful sales professional is persistence. Now that I've more thoroughly researched your company, I don't intend to give up trying until I am successful in joining one of the best sales teams in the business and one of the best organizations in town!

My sales background is strong. In each of the last four years, in two different sales positions, I have exceeded my sales goals by 10% or more. I attribute this success to superior closing skills and dedication to every step of the sales process.

Since January, my performance has been measured by how well I continue selling after the initial sale is made. Customers come to me after they have decided to purchase a new car, and I sell them financing plans and add-on features and services. By carefully listening to my customers' needs and recommending the add-ons that are right for them, I have sold more extended service plans and dealer-installed stereo systems than anyone in my position in the last five years.

I'm confident I can deliver similar results for Alpha Omega, and I am eager to be part of your team.

If you have any questions before our meeting, please contact me by phone or email. Otherwise, I look forward to seeing you at 3 pm on Friday.

Sincerely,

Darryl T. Poston

attachment

Sample Cover Letter 3: After an Interview (Ted Markham)

Comments: This letter shows how you might follow up after an interview and make a pitch for solving a problem—even when no job formally exists. In this example, the writer suggests that he can use his skills to solve a specific problem he uncovered during his conversation with the employer. Although it never occurs to many job seekers to set up an interview where there appears to be no job opening, jobs are created as a result of such interviews.

Ted Markham

7529 Old Bay Boulevard, Pinellas Park, FL 33781
727-249-8349 — tedmarkham@tampabay.rr.com

April 30, 2005

Shannon Edwards
Vice President, Marketing & Community Relations
Highland Hospital
2945 Hospital Road
Tampa, FL 33605

Dear Ms. Edwards:

Thank you for taking time to meet with me on Wednesday. I was impressed with everything I learned about Highland Hospital—you have just the culture, challenges, and people that I find create the most satisfying work environment. I realize you don't have a position available right now for someone with my skills, but I would like to keep in touch and share some ideas with you from time to time.

I have been thinking about one of the challenges we discussed. Your need for enhancing ties with current physicians as well as recruiting new doctors matches the situation I faced at Sarasota Regional Hospital. By tapping into our strong network of volunteers and board members, I was able to improve our communications with physicians and get better results in our recruiting initiatives. If you have an interest, I would be happy to share more details of what we did and how effective it was.

Thank you, also, for suggesting I speak with Roger Midland at South Coastal Health Center. I have a call in to him, and I will follow up with you next week to let you know how our conversation goes. If there is anything I can do for you in the meantime, please call; the best number to reach me is my cell phone, 727-249-8349.

Sincerely,

Ted Markham

P.S. A copy of my resume is attached for your files—or to pass along to someone who you think might be interested in talking to me. As I mentioned, I am eager to make a move within the next six to nine months.

Sample Cover Letter 4: No Interview Is Scheduled (Brett Samuelson)

Comments: This letter makes an immediate connection with the recipient by mentioning a referral from a professional association. This type of connection can be an excellent source of contacts and job leads. Note that the writer will call again to arrange an appointment. This is an effective message because it leaves the ball firmly in the job seeker's court. Instead of relying on a busy executive to pick up the phone, the person with the most at stake (you, the job seeker) should persist in seeking a telephone conversation and ultimately an in-person meeting.

BRETT SAMUELSON

295 Skyline Drive, Ft. Thomas, KY 41015
Home 859-349-9076 • Mobile 859-208-0987 • brett@samuelson.com

April 30, 2005

Mr. Thomas Elder
Director of Marketing
Sabatino Specialties, Inc.
259 Vine Street
Cincinnati, OH 45202

Dear Mr. Elder:

Rachel Koehler (current president of the Cincinnati Chapter of the American Marketing Association) suggested that I contact you about marketing opportunities that you may know of in your role as chairman of the Cincinnati Incubator marketing board. I hope you received my voice-mail message on Monday—as promised, I am following up with more information.

I recently married and relocated to the Cincinnati area, and I am eager to find a young technology company that needs an experienced marketing professional to help introduce its innovations to various business markets.

My background and interests are a good fit for emerging high-tech companies. Since completing my MBA, I've helped two fledgling software developers gain solid traction in their markets. I understand how to position and present new technology concepts to business audiences (emphasizing business benefits, not just technology advances).

I will call you early next week to follow up. I appreciate any ideas, referrals, or assistance you can offer!

Sincerely,

Brett Samuelson

P.S.   The enclosed resume provides more detailed information about my experience, expertise, and track record.

Writing Cover Letters to People You Don't Know

If it is not practical to directly contact a prospective employer by phone or some other method, it is acceptable to send a resume and cover letter. This approach makes sense in some situations, such as if you are moving to a distant location or responding to a blind ad offering only a post office box number.

In other instances, you might have tried but cannot connect with the person you are writing to. Because your time and other resources are limited, it does not make sense for you to spend hours pursuing contact information for a newspaper ad. Neither do you want to ignore these opportunities. We recommend that you make one or two phone calls to try make a connection and customize your letter. But if you are unsuccessful, it is better to respond with a generic letter than not to respond at all. To make these letters as effective as possible, try to find something you have in common with the person or company you are contacting. You will see some examples of how this is done in the following sample letters.

Note: *It is a fact that most people do not find their jobs through newspaper ads or Internet postings. The reality is that only about 15 percent of people find jobs through these two methods combined, according to a survey conducted by the* New York Times *in 2002. Job seekers who spend most of their time sending out dozens (or hundreds) of letters and resumes in response to ads often feel frustrated when they get no response. Not only that, their search takes longer than necessary. We want to repeat our recommendation that you write to people you know or people you can get to know. You will get a better response to your letters, and your job search activities will be much more purposeful and satisfying.*

Sample Cover Letter 5: Response to a Want Ad (Antonio Ruiz)

Comments: This letter does a good job of outlining the candidate's credentials as relevant to the position advertised. The bullet points give the reader a quick overview of his qualifications; then more detail is provided if the reader cares to know more before turning to the resume. Note the explanation for relocating to Florida—and note how prominently this is displayed, directly under his name at the top of the page. This can help ease an employer's concerns about the cost of bringing in someone from outside the area.

Because this letter was written in response to a blind ad, Antonio cannot state when and how he will be following up. In cases like this, a less assertive closing must be used, but it is still a good idea to ask for further contact.

Antonio Ruiz

Mobile: 317-218-4594   **Relocating to Florida May 2005**   antonioruiz@att.com

Re: Licensed Contractor Position, *Miami Herald,* April 27, 2005

With in-depth construction management experience and a 30-year record of never missing a project-completion date, I have proven skills and a track record of performance that can benefit your company as a Licensed Contractor.

In brief, I offer

- Expertise in all facets of commercial/industrial and residential construction
- State of Florida General Contractor license (fully up to date with annual CEUs)
- Record of 100% on-time, on-budget project completion
- High quality standards and ability to get top results from contractor crews
- Proven dependability, integrity, and dedication to customer satisfaction

As a partner in a small construction company, I have managed every stage of a project, from preparing bids to handing over keys to new owners. Through active daily oversight on every project, I eliminate problems such as subcontractor miscommunication, faulty construction, blueprint misinterpretation, and carelessness. My relationships with subcontractors (both managers and crew) have always been excellent, and I am able to create the teamwork necessary for successful, profitable projects.

I have been a regular visitor to Florida for more than 10 years and now plan to make the state my permanent home. The position with your company sounds like an excellent fit for my skills and track record. May we schedule a time to talk?

Sincerely,

Antonio Ruiz

Enclosure: Resume

Sample Cover Letter 6: Unsolicited Resume Sent to Obtain an Interview (Jennifer Tolles)

Comments: In this letter, the candidate makes an immediate connection by referring to a recent news article that featured the school system to which she is applying. Her bullet points make additional connections to what she learned about the school district. This helps send the message that she understands and fits into the unique culture of that organization. Notice how she indicates that she will call in hopes of setting up a meeting. Although she could not make a connection beforehand, she will work diligently to establish one after the fact.

Jennifer Tolles

75 Bolivar Terrace, Reading, MA 01867
jennifertee@aol.com
781-592-3409

April 30, 2005

Dr. Mark B. Cronin, Superintendent
Belmont Public Schools
644 Pleasant Street
Belmont, MA 02478

Dear Dr. Cronin:

Your school district's reputation for *excellence in education*—described so vividly in the recent *New England Journal of Elementary Education*—has prompted me to forward my resume for consideration for fall teaching positions. In addition to strong professional qualifications, you will find that I also have the intangible personal qualities that fit your culture and enable me to truly make a difference to the children I teach.

Please consider my qualifications:

- Recent bachelor's degree and Massachusetts teaching certification, grades 1–8.

- Year-long teaching experience as an LD Tutor for elementary and high school students—experience adapting classroom materials for individual students, delivering individual and group lessons, working collaboratively with classroom teachers, and promoting a positive learning environment for my students.

- Diverse field-teaching experiences (grades 1, 4, and 6); successful experience planning and delivering integrated lessons that sparked students' interest, creativity, and desire to learn.

- Keen respect for each individual child and appreciation for the differences among us.

- A highly effective classroom-management style that creates an environment in which all children can learn.

I will call you within a few days to see when it might be convenient to meet. Thank you for your consideration.

Sincerely,

Jennifer Tolles

enclosure

Sample Cover Letter 7: No Interview Is Scheduled (Tyler Wilson-Dooley)

Comments: This letter is shown in an e-mail format and is a response to an online posting. This candidate tries to set himself apart from perhaps hundreds of candidates by emphasizing his eager interest in near-space exploration along with intangible qualities that will make him a good employee.

Subject: Software Engineer—Monster.com posting SW-43902

Your posting describes needs that are a near-perfect fit for my career experience and interests. In brief, my qualifications include the following:

** Programming and scripting skills in JAVA, JavaScript, Perl, and C.
** Extensive development experience in multiple environments and methodologies.
** Leadership roles in the development of secure content managers.
** Project management experience and the ability to bring projects in on time and on budget.

But it is my passionate interest in near-space exploration that sets me apart from other candidates with similar skills and experience. I am extremely interested in putting my skills to work in the atmosphere of exploration that characterizes the Jet Propulsion Laboratory.

I can easily schedule a phone interview at your convenience and would be very willing to travel to Pasadena for further discussions. I am confident I will convince you that I have the technical skills you're looking for as well as the intangible qualities—enthusiasm, energy, dedication, sense of mission, and intellectual curiosity—that characterize your best employees.

Thank you.

Sincerely,

Tyler Wilson-Dooley

Key Points: Chapter 1

Here's a summary of the key points of this chapter:

- Whenever possible, send your cover letter and resume to someone you know.

- Try to arrange an interview before you send your cover letter and resume.

- Don't limit your job search to responding to published or posted openings. Not only will the competition be fierce, you will be missing about 85 percent of job opportunities!

- Don't waste your time and money sending form letters to hundreds of unknown people or companies.

- Always customize the content of your letter for the specific person, organization, or opportunity. Make a connection between what they are looking for and what you have to offer.

- Keep the ball in your court by informing your reader how and when you will follow up—then be sure to do so.

Chapter 2

Write Your Own
15-Minute Cover Letter

We promised you an easy-to-use, foolproof system to write cover letters that are individual, personal, and effective—in about 15 minutes. In this chapter we'll lead you through the process step by step. Along with explanations and examples, we'll give you some tools and exercises that you can use to rapidly generate material for your letters. Then we'll show you how to put it all together for a polished, professional presentation.

Here are the eight start-to-finish steps to write and send your own cover letter:

- Step 1: Create Your Format
- Step 2: Add the Basics
- Step 3: State Why You're Writing and Get the Reader's Attention
- Step 4: Add Relevant, Compelling Information
- Step 5: Close with an Action Statement
- Step 6: Proofread and Polish
- Step 7: Choose the Transmission Method (Mail or E-mail)
- Step 8: Send and Follow Up

As we expand on each of these steps in the following sections, you will find examples of different ways to present the information. In some cases we have created worksheets for you to use to develop your material, as well as "quick tips" and other suggestions for making the process as smooth and painless as possible.

If you spend time completing all of the exercises, it will take you more than 15 minutes to write your first cover letter. But after just a few times, you should have enough material and a firm grasp of the process so that you'll be able to move rapidly through each step, creating, reviewing, and sending cover letters quickly and easily for each unique opportunity you uncover during your search.

Step 1: Create Your Format

You can use a Wizard or template from your word-processing program or copy the heading and font choices from your resume. Either way, start out by creating a new word-processing file and showing your name, address, telephone number(s), and e-mail address at the top of the page. This information does not have to be extremely large and prominent, but you do want to make it easy for readers to contact you right away if they are interested in your background.

For the body of your letter, we recommend a fairly conservative font that is easy to read. Times New Roman, Arial, Book Antiqua, Bookman, Garamond, and Tahoma are attractive fonts that are found on most PCs. If you want to use a more decorative or distinctive font for your name, go ahead and do so. Just be sure it is not too playful or hard to read.

> **Tip:** A cover letter sent as an e-mail message requires a different format than a traditional paper letter. In Step 7 we address this issue and provide complete details for converting your word-processing file to an e-mail message. For now, we suggest that you follow the formatting steps outlined here so that you will have the print format ready to go when you need it.

To create a cohesive, highly professional image, be sure that your cover letter mimics the font and style choices of your resume.

Save your document with a distinctive name that will allow you to access the file quickly when you need it. You might label it according to the organization name or person you are writing to. Or if you are starting out by creating a generic letter that you plan to customize for individual letters throughout your search, be sure your file name reflects this fact.

Following are three different ways to format a cover letter. There is no rule for what's right or what's best—use your judgment and choose something you like, whether one of these or one of your own. We advise that you keep your format professional looking and that you use something that is easy for you to reproduce time after time as you write customized cover letters throughout your search.

Format Example 1

Sandra Smithers

ssmithers@cinci.rr.com

Home 513-249-8409 • Mobile 513-606-3909
7529 Fallen Oak Lane, Loveland, OH 45140

Date

Mr. Rafael Montoya
Accounting Manager
West Side Realty
2509 Central Parkway
Cincinnati, OH 45204

Dear Mr. Montoya:

Opening paragraph

Paragraph of relevant, compelling information

- Bullet point 1
- Bullet point 2
- Bullet point 3

Closing paragraph

Sincerely,

Sandra Smithers

attachment: resume

FONT NOTES:
Text font: Times New Roman, 11 pt.
Headline (name) font: Verdana Bold, 18 pt.

Format Example 2

STEVEN ADAMS

11099 Desert Sands Drive
Tempe, AZ 27317
827-876-0043
steveadams@aol.com

Date

Ellen Masterson, R.N.
Director of Nursing
Mercy Hospital
7450 Hospital Drive
Phoenix, AZ 27312

Dear Ms. Masterson:

Opening paragraph

Paragraph of relevant, compelling information

Paragraph of relevant, compelling information

Closing paragraph

Sincerely yours,

Steven Adams

Enclosure

FONT NOTES:
Text font: Arial, 11 pt.
Headline (name) font: Arial Black, 18 pt., small caps

Format Example 3

DALE GELMAN

phone: (203) 549-0929 • *cell:* (203) 303-1276 • *e-mail:* DALE@SNET.NET
residence: 459 ELM STREET • NORTH GUILFORD, CT
mailing address: P.O. BOX 750 • MADISON, CT 06443-0750

Date

Ms. Chris Andenoro
District Manager
Cintas Services
75 Shoreline Industrial Park
Branford, CT 06473

Dear Ms. Andenoro:

Opening paragraph
(first line of each paragraph indented)

Paragraph of relevant, compelling information

Paragraph of relevant, compelling information

Closing paragraph

Sincerely yours,

Dale Gelman

Enclosure

FONT NOTES:
Style adapted to match "Contemporary Resume" template in Microsoft Word.
Text font: Garamond, 11 pt.
Headline (name) font: Garamond, 22 pt., all caps, spacing expanded 4 pt.

Step 2: Add the Basics

A few lines below your contact information, type today's date, then space down two or three lines and type the name, title, and address of the person you're writing to. If there is any question about this information, make a phone call to verify it. It is especially important to use the person's correct name and title and to spell everything correctly!

Two spaces below this "inside address," write a formal salutation, such as this:

Dear Mr. Singh:

Be sure to use a colon, not a comma, after the salutation (this is the proper punctuation for formal business correspondence such as initial cover letters; thank-you notes and other follow-up letters can use a comma instead). Do not address the individual by first name unless it is someone you know well.

Step 3: State Why You're Writing and Get the Reader's Attention

The first paragraph of your letter should let your reader know why you are writing. Are you confirming a scheduled meeting and sending along a resume? Have you been referred by a mutual acquaintance? Are you following up on a phone or e-mail message? Were you prompted to write by a newspaper advertisement or an interesting article about the company? Don't be mysterious! Share this information up front so that your reader can place your letter in the proper context.

For the most compelling opening of all—the one that will get immediate attention—refer to your prior conversation or interview appointment, or "drop" the name of the person who referred you. If you don't have a referral and you haven't been able to make a prior connection, try to make your opening sentence interesting enough to draw the reader into the rest of your letter. We don't suggest that you get too clever or "gimmicky," but do avoid dry, overused introductions such as "I am writing to inquire about positions

> **Tip:** *Remember, the most compelling opening is a follow-up to your initial contact or the name of a person who referred you. Personal connection beats a clever opening every day of the week!*

with your company." Instead, write something that will make your reader want to know more about you and how you can help with a specific problem or challenge. Here are a few ideas for doing that:

Quote a Relevant Article

I was interested to read in Business Monthly *that San Marcos Manufacturing plans to expand its Asian operations to Vietnam and China. With seven years of experience launching production (both plant start-up and supplier development) in both of these countries, I can help make this important venture successful for you.*

Quote a Recent Industry Statistic

Health care workers are in the shortest supply since the 1950s, according to a recent article in Health Careers. *If you are experiencing this shortage at County General, I believe you will be interested in my qualifications as a surgical technician and my strong desire to join your team.*

Quote Your Contact Directly

"Companies succeed by hiring the right people—people who want to make a difference, not just do a job." When I read this statement in your interview that was recently published in the Chicago Tribune, *I knew that General Widget was a great fit for my energy and passion as well as my skills as a machinist.*

Lead with One of Your Most Startling and Relevant Successes

Under my leadership as Sales & Marketing VP for MoneyMakers, we grew market share from 10% to 24% on a shoestring budget. I'd like to speak with you about opportunities where I can deliver this level of sales results for Acme Funds.

As you become aware of industry statistics, interesting articles, and quotes that can help you create a compelling opening paragraph, make a note of them. This worksheet will become a ready source of information so that you can quickly put together an interesting opening statement that relates to the company and its specific needs, plans, and interests.

WORKSHEET 1: MATERIAL FOR OPENING PARAGRAPH

Industry Statistics

Statistic _____

Source _____

Statistic _____

Source _____

Statistic _____

Source _____

Statistic _____

Source _____

Interesting Articles

Article title _____

Key points _____

_____

_____

Source _____

Article title _____

Key points _____

_____

_____

Source _____

(continued)

(continued)

Article title _____

Key points _____

_____

_____

Source _____

Article title _____

Key points _____

_____

_____

Source _____

Quotes

Quote _____

_____

Speaker and source _____

Quote _____

_____

Speaker and source _____

Quote _____

_____

Speaker and source _____

Quote _____

_____

Speaker and source _____

Step 4: Share Information Relevant to the Reader's Needs

Here is the heart of your letter: the middle paragraph or two, or the brief list of bullet points, that tells the reader something about you that is relevant to his or her needs. Employers are not interested in you for your sake but rather because of what you can bring to the organization. This might sound harsh, but businesspeople have an obligation to improve the success of their organization. If you consistently show how you can help them do this—in your resume, your cover letter, your interviews, and all aspects of your job search—they will be much more motivated to talk to you than if you focus on *your* needs and interests.

Let's say you are a salesperson who is interested in working for a company that pays generous commissions. There's nothing wrong with that—you certainly have the right to be interested in your compensation. But sharing this with employers will not convince them that you have their needs at heart. Instead, share how you have been successful in past sales positions, and tell them you are confident and comfortable working with a commission pay structure. This communicates that you will perform equally well for them and that you're not afraid to base your pay on your own performance. Do you see the difference? Of course, you do need to have a clear understanding of your personal needs and wishes, but you should not make your interests the heart of your cover letter. Focus on the employer and your value to the organization. Your cover letters will be much more effective.

If your cover letter relates to a specific job opening, you can use the job description to interpret the employer's needs. Add in your knowledge of the job function, the company, and the industry, and you will have quite a bit of information about what the employer is looking for—what kind of problems you would be hired to solve. In this section of your letter, you will show how you can solve those problems and how you have done so in the past.

Example Job Postings and Corresponding Cover Letter Sections

Here is an example of a job posting, followed by the middle section of a cover letter that responds to the employer's needs as stated in the posting.

Customer Service Associate

If you love talking with people, solving problems, and working with prestigious clients, this position is for you. You will assist employees from a growing client list with questions about their benefit plans and help them solve complex issues related to their health, savings, and retirement plans.

You will have an opportunity to use your
— Excellent communication skills
— Computer knowledge
— Analytical skills
— Problem-solving capabilities

Minimum requirements include
— A stable work history
— At least two years of continuous customer service experience
— Knowledge of Windows and Internet

My experience in the fast-paced environment of a technical call center is directly relevant to your needs. For the past three years, I have helped employees from all departments and all locations of our global company resolve various technical problems. This requires not only excellent technical skills, but patience, attentive listening, and the ability to explain technical solutions to non-technical workers. My efforts have been so successful, I have twice earned "Customer Service Rep of the Quarter" from among more than 300 people at our call center.

Note how this brief paragraph addresses the key requirements of the position and also provides evidence of this candidate's ability to do the job well. There is no mention of the candidate's concerns or interests—whether for higher pay, a more flexible work schedule, a more understanding boss, a lower-stress work environment, or any other factor that is not important to the employer's needs.

Here is another example.

Transportation Manager: Excellent career opportunity! Individual will be responsible for implementing and developing cost-saving programs, in addition to improving load efficiencies and transportation processes.

Requirements:
**3–5 years transportation supervisory experience
**3–5 years transportation industry experience servicing large retail accounts
**10 years domestic transportation (Rail, LTL, TL carriers)
**Working knowledge of U.S. Transportation regulations and comfortable with transportation practices in all U.S. regions
**Documented success of improving cost and efficiencies of transportation operations

Educational Requirement:
**Bachelor's degree in Transportation, Logistics, or Business

Computer Knowledge:
**Proficient with MS Office
** Transportation Management Software

Interpersonal Skills:
**Success in a team-based environment, including leadership and employee development
**Demonstrated successful interaction with internal and external customers

---

- *As Transportation Manager for Ames' Midwest Region, in just over a year I cut hundreds of thousands of dollars from operating costs, improved productivity 12%, and contributed to the division's first profitable quarter ever.*

- *For automotive-supplier Klein Auto Systems, I implemented a new loading system that improved efficiency more than 35% and enabled us to achieve same-day supply status for our top 10 accounts.*

I'm confident I can deliver similar results for your organization.

In brief, I am an experienced transportation manager and project leader. I understand and apply state-of-the-art methodologies for continuous improvement of the distribution process; yet I realize that it is people who ultimately deliver results, and I am strongly focused on building relationships with employees, managers, suppliers, and customers as a primary tool for business success.

In this example you can see how the candidate shared documented successes in the areas that are most important to the employer. The last paragraph expands on the less-tangible qualities of leadership and teamwork that are also cited by the employer as essential skills.

Some job seekers prefer a side-by-side comparison of their qualifications with every requirement called for in a job description. Known as the "T-style" cover letter, this format makes it easy for employers to quickly ascertain that you have the basic job requirements.

CRITICAL CARE REGISTERED NURSES (ICU, EMERGENCY, CARDIAC)

Responsibilities
Responsible for coordinating clinical care of patient. Integrate all health care providers to ensure high quality patient/family outcomes, and establish a consistent and accountable relationship with patient/family. Key responsibilities include, but are not limited to, initiation and development of the plan of care, patient/family education, utilization management, and discharge planning.

Qualifications:
· Licensure: Registered Nurse, State of Hawaii
· Diploma or Associate Degree in Nursing; Baccalaureate Degree in Nursing preferred
· Current BLS/HCP card in all areas; ACLS, NALS and/or PALS in designated areas
· Ability to read, write, speak, and understand English effectively

---

With more than five years of experience coordinating critical care for patients in multiple hospital departments (ICU, NICU, ER, Cardiac Care Unit), I offer strong qualifications that are an excellent match for your needs.

You Require...	I Offer...
Licensure	Registered Nurse, State of Hawaii (since 2003)
Degree	BSN, University of Illinois, 1998
Certifications	Current BLS/HCP card; NALS and PALS certification
English Language	Native English speaker; also developing fluency in Hawaiian

---

While easy to peruse, this format is not always the best strategy. One problem is that it can shine a glaring light on areas in which you are not as strong as other candidates, and therefore make it easy for the employer to eliminate you from consideration. If you like this style, we recommend that you use it only when you are a perfect match (or better) for every qualification the employer is seeking.

Of course, you will not always be able to refer to a job description when writing your cover letters. In those instances, do your best to determine what the employer's most pressing concerns are, and address those in your cover letter. If no position exists, refer to what you know about the company and the industry. Here is an example of the middle section of a cover letter that does just that.

> *Today's manufacturing economy presents many challenges. To stay competitive, plants must constantly become more efficient. I believe that the best way to accomplish this is by involving all employees in the improvement initiatives. When production workers are invested and involved, they put their heart and soul into meeting (and often exceeding) goals.*
>
> *I put this philosophy into action as production supervisor at Western Widgets. To keep our costs competitive, we were challenged to increase efficiency by 10% without an investment in technology. I brainstormed with all of our production staff, and we broke down into teams to test three of their ideas. With a little competition, everyone was motivated to make their idea work the best. As a result, we implemented two of the ideas on the production line, increased efficiency 12%, and rewarded every worker for his or her contribution.*

Note: *We don't believe it's essential that you compare your qualifications point-by-point with every requirement in a job description. Remember, your cover letter accompanies your resume, which provides much more detail. The main purpose of your cover letter is simply to create interest in talking with you to find out more. If you hit on your most important qualifications and most significant contributions—always in areas of interest to the people you are writing to—then you will pique their interest and motivate them to look at your resume and ultimately pick up the phone to contact you for an interview.*

If your cover letter can expand on a specific problem you've already discussed in your initial phone call, so much the better. With this strategy you show employers that you listened, understood their concerns, and already have ideas for solutions. Here is an example.

> *In our discussion on Wednesday you mentioned the high level of absenteeism in the call center. I have some ideas and some experience that might help—for example, at Techline we were experiencing absenteeism as high as 20% that really hurt our response times. We set up a series of incentives that increased for every week, month, and quarter of perfect attendance. Employees knew they had control over their bonus payments and therefore took responsibility for their own attendance.*

> *Not only that, we added team bonuses as well, so that team members encouraged their peers to come to work. As a result, our attendance improved to a steady 95%, we cut 30 seconds from our average response time, and the increased productivity more than covered the cost of the bonuses.*

Show Results and Be Specific

The theme that runs through all of these examples is *results*. Employers are interested in applicants who have performed well in their past positions, and sharing specific examples will help them understand how you can add value to their organization.

Another key point is that the most credible and powerful examples are specific, not general. An employer might advertise for someone with "five years of sales experience in the medical industry," but if you have called ahead, learned more about the company, and know that they want someone to sell disposable medical products to hospitals, you can make your example much more specific and relevant: "I have five years of successful experience (averaging 125% of quota) in sales of disposable medical products to hospital purchasing departments."

Consider the difference in impact when we add specifics and results to straightforward qualifications statements:

Before	After
My experience includes leading technical teams and projects for major clients of our consulting firm.	My track record reflects 100% on-time delivery of critical client projects, leading 5- to 10-person technical teams implementing enterprise software (primarily SAP) for client companies such as Acme, XYZ, and Worldwide.
I have marketing experience with several retail chains and an excellent grasp of merchandising.	At Federated, I developed marketing and merchandising strategies for the Southwest Region that resulted in 20% more traffic and a 12% increase in same-store sales.
My background in the construction industry is broad. I am knowledgeable rough and finish carpentry, electrical, HVAC, and plumbing for projects of all sizes.	As construction supervisor, I directed the activities of all of our subcontractors (carpentry, electrical, HVAC, and in plumbing) and was able to create a true teamwork environment. In fact, on the $140 million Camp Building project, we set the lowest record in our company's 10-year history for "lost days" due to subcontractor scheduling and material problems.

In all of these examples, it is important to understand that the specifics provided are directly relevant to the employer's needs. For your letters to be powerful and effective, you must relate your experiences and achievements to the specific concerns that you have been able to uncover before writing your letter.

Yet it's true that most organizations have similar needs in common. Every business is concerned about making money (both revenue and profit). Every business, government, and not-for profit organization would like to improve its efficiency, productivity, and customer service. When you write about your successes and experiences for one organization, you will often be able to use those same statements in another letter, perhaps slightly editing to customize your letter to the second organization's circumstances.

Create a Library of Success Stories and Experience Statements

Wouldn't it be easier to write your cover letters quickly if you had a resource where you could quickly review, select, and then edit this important "middle section" material? We recommend that you create just such a resource.

Every time you write a cover letter, copy your success stories and achievement statements (the "middle section" of the letter) into a separate document where all of these sections are stored. After you've written three or four letters, rather than starting from scratch each time, go first to your "library" and see if one of your prior sections is applicable for the new letter you're about to write.

It will be even more helpful if you tag each of your library entries with keywords that relate to the specific competency, success, or experience it illustrates. You can use a worksheet like the one we provide in this section, or simply create a word-processing file where you store all of this information for easy access.

Here are two worksheets—one blank, for your use (you may copy as many of these worksheets as you need), and one filled in for a sales representative. The filled-in sample shows competencies in a variety of areas—individual performance, team leadership, training, customer problem-solving, and territory management and growth—that this individual will want to highlight in various cover letters, depending on the specific opportunity and the needs and challenges of the employer.

> **Tip:** For your cover letters, you can expand on many of the results, examples, and success stories that are in your resume. However, it's never a good idea to transfer information word-for-word from your resume to your cover letter. Be sure that you say something different about the accomplishment, add more details, blend two or three accomplishments from your resume into one story for your cover letter, or otherwise change the information so that your cover letter is not a carbon copy of your resume. If your resume is not filled with strong accomplishments, see chapter 5 for our suggestions on how to add power and meaning to your resume.

WORKSHEET 2: COVER LETTER LIBRARY
(MIDDLE SECTION)

Competency/Quality/Experience:

_____

Example _____

_____

_____

_____

_____

Competency/Quality/Experience:

_____

Example _____

_____

_____

_____

_____

Competency/Quality/Experience:

_____

Example _____

_____

_____

_____

_____

_____

(continued)

(continued)

Competency/Quality/Experience:

_____

Example _____

_____

_____

_____

_____

Competency/Quality/Experience:

_____

Example _____

_____

_____

_____

_____

WORKSHEET 2: COVER LETTER LIBRARY (MIDDLE SECTION)—COMPLETED EXAMPLE

Competency/Quality/Experience:

Sales success (team leadership)

Example: As District Manager for Super Foods, I led my 6-person team to #1 in our region. We held the top spot for 4 years, and during that time I retained everyone on the team at a time when demand was high and they were getting several calls a week from competitors, inviting them to jump ship.

Competency/Quality/Experience:

Sales success (individual performance)

Example: Managing a new sales territory for a start-up food distributor, I was quickly successful because of my cold-calling and relationship-building skills:

- #1 in my region, every year
- #2 in the nation, 1997
- 100% sales growth every year for 4 consecutive years

Competency/Quality/Experience:

Customer problem-solving skills

Example: I understand that long-term sales success relies on solving customer problems. That is my specialty. For example, with Super Foods I developed Midwest Grocers from a $10K to a $100K account in one year by solving a long-standing problem they had with perishable foods spoilage.

(continued)

(continued)

Competency/Quality/Experience:

Territory management and growth

> Example: Having managed territories as large as three states, I understand the importance of good planning and regular sales visits. This often pays off in unexpected ways! For instance, on a regular quarterly visit to my smallest customer, I learned that they were experiencing growth of their Hispanic customer base, and I secured an additional order for new products that increased this account by 25%. With this knowledge, I cold-called two other stores in the area and gained $200K in new business.

Competency/Quality/Experience:

Sales training

Example: After just one year with the company, I was asked to field-train struggling reps. Keeping my territory at 120% to plan, I helped them excel also:

- Reps I trained showed an immediate 10%–20% growth in sales.

- Every one of them exceeded plan that year—some for the first time ever.

- Our region soared from #10 to #2 in the nation.

Two Quick Tips

Here are two quick tips to keep in mind as you write your cover letters:

1. **Keep your cover letters brief.** You do not need to tell employers everything about yourself or include every one of your qualifications in the letter. Choose the most important, most compelling, and most relevant information for that particular circumstance. Hit the highlights. If you interest your readers and you grab their attention by showing how you can help solve their problems, they will review your resume or call you to ask for any additional details they need.

2. **Keep your cover letters readable.** Paragraphs should be no longer than four or five lines. Otherwise, the text is too dense and the letter is uninviting. If necessary, break overly long paragraphs into multiple paragraphs, or separate some of the information into bullet points that make it easy for the reader to quickly skim your letter.

Step 5: Close with an Action Statement

Thus far, your cover letter has opened on a strong, personal note, then gone on to include relevant and compelling information in the middle section. Now you must keep the momentum going by closing with an assertive yet polite request to advance to the next step.

We do not recommend that you leave it up to the employer to contact you. After all, your job search is the number-one priority for no one but you. Close on a positive note and let the employer know you desire further contact. Better yet, tell the employer you will call to follow up, and be sure that you keep this promise.

In your closing, don't lose your focus on how you can help an employer solve problems. Instead of simply stating what you want, try to include information about what you can do for the employer. Here are a few examples:

Mr. Smith, I look forward to meeting with you on Monday (I'll be there at 10:00 sharp) and sharing my ideas for your Northeast distribution center.

Thank you for the opportunity to meet with you on Friday. I am looking forward to learning more about your needs and exploring how my skills and experience can be of value to you.

I would appreciate the opportunity to meet with you to learn more about the challenge of expanding your Asian manufacturing capabilities. I will call you early next week to see when it might be convenient to get together, and in the meantime I will put together a few notes and ideas from my experiences in China and Korea.

Assertive vs. Aggressive

We recommend an assertive closing, but we don't recommend that you get too aggressive. Keep your closing polite, positive, and pleasant. It is always better to request than to demand. Consider the difference:

Assertive:

I will call within the next few days to see if we can schedule a time to meet. I'd like to share my ideas for improving the productivity of your field technicians.

Aggressive:

I will call you at 10:00 on Tuesday. Please be available to discuss my ideas for improving the productivity of your field technicians.

Assertive:

I eagerly await your ideas and suggestions. I will call on Thursday in hopes of setting up a brief meeting at a time that is convenient for you.

Aggressive:

Your support is important for my job search, and I eagerly await all the leads you can give me. I will call on Thursday to see what names you have collected thus far.

When Follow-Up Isn't Possible

Sometimes you might be sending cover letters and resumes in response to "blind" ads and you won't know who is receiving your letter—or perhaps even what company it is going to. In those cases, your follow-up is limited—you cannot promise to call, for example. So how do you keep your closing assertive and action-oriented? Here are a few ideas:

Because my qualifications appear to be an excellent fit for your needs, I look forward to the opportunity for an interview. You can reach me most easily on my cell phone (212-489-5612).

I look forward to learning more about this interesting opportunity and exploring the fit with my experience. I would be pleased to answer any quick questions you have by telephone (212-489-5612), and, of course, I'd like to meet with you at greater length in person. I am confident I can help your organization achieve its goals.

May we schedule a time to talk soon? I am a strong candidate for this position and would like to share my ideas with you while learning more about your current and future challenges.

In most cases, your closing will be one paragraph long. Be brief, action-oriented, and focused on your ability to add value.

In some instances, you will want to include additional information before closing your letter. You might wish to convey your reasons for making a change, some personal information that makes you an exceptionally strong fit for the organization or the opportunity, or perhaps your intention to relocate. You do not need to share your entire personal history with your readers, but on occasion this added information will make you a stronger candidate or erase a concern in the employer's mind.

Let's explore these scenarios in more detail.

Reason for Making a Change

While you do not need to share this information, it might be beneficial to do so. Let's say you are leaving your current job after a very short period of time. An employer might be concerned about "job hopping." If you can eliminate this concern right up front, why not do so?

Shortly after I started my current job six months ago, the company owner passed away very unexpectedly. This caused enormous change for the family-owned business, and they have decided to downsize to just one facility and keep the longest-tenured staff.

My current position is very satisfying, and my manager has said she has never seen anyone come up to speed so quickly. But my spouse recently was offered a promotion to 3M headquarters in Minneapolis, so we have decided to relocate to afford her this tremendous opportunity.

Although I have not been actively looking—I have been in my current position for less than a year and find it very satisfying—when Dale told me about this position, I could not pass up the opportunity to return to my hometown of Kansas City. My roots are deep in the Midwest where most of my family resides.

Relevant Personal Information

Your cover letters should be customized for each specific opportunity or circumstance. In some cases you will have a strong personal reason for targeting a particular company or industry. Why not share this information if it helps the employer connect with you?

Having been a model-train buff since childhood, I am very excited about coming to work for Lionel. I know that my passion for your products, as well as my expertise in sales and marketing, will help me become one of your top performers.

My passion for teaching special-needs children stems from my own personal experience as the sister and cousin of two developmentally disabled individuals. I have learned firsthand what a difference it makes when they are properly taught and encouraged to be the best that they can be. For me, this is not just a job; it is a consuming interest.

As a part-time writer myself, I am enamored of the world of books and can think of nothing more satisfying than working in a bookstore. My knowledge of science fiction (even the most obscure authors and titles!) will enable me to be a resource to your customers and other staff.

Intention to Relocate

If you are applying for jobs outside your area, the employer might be concerned that you will expect a relocation package. Sometimes these are just not available, and for that reason employers sometimes will interview only candidates who live in the immediate area. You might be able to put yourself in the running if you communicate that you intend to relocate, and at your own expense.

I will be relocating to Chicago early in September, when my husband begins medical school at Northwestern. We are excited about our new city, and I will be ready to begin my next career opportunity as soon as we move.

Although I currently live in Sarasota, I am in the process of relocating to Austin, where I grew up. I do not expect relocation assistance, as I will be making this move on my own within the next few weeks.

Disclosing Salary Information

With our recommended approach of direct contact with people you know rather than massive ad responses, you do not need to worry about disclosing salary information in your cover letters. The question might come up in your interviews, and you will need to be prepared to answer the question, but for the most part you can appropriately ignore this issue in your cover letters.

At times, though, it is quite likely that you will be responding to ads, and some of the ads might request or even demand salary information. What should you do?

We recommend that you not share your salary history or salary requirements with employers at this stage. After all, you do not know much about the position. If it is a blind ad, you have not even been able to research the company or the industry. Why should you disclose information that can work against you whether it is too high or too low?

Instead, we suggest that you choose one of these options:

- **Ignore it.** Research shows that employers will—almost 100 percent of the time—look at your resume anyway if they think you have the skills they are looking for.

- **Provide a range.** You might feel more comfortable responding to the request in some way. If so, we recommend that you first conduct salary research to learn average salaries for the position, and then state your salary requirement in the form of a range. "I understand that typical salaries for this type of position are in the mid forties to mid fifties range, and I anticipate a comparable salary from your company."

- **Respond if required.** Sometimes you will see an ad that states you "must" include salary information or your application will not be accepted. In these cases, you don't have much choice. Again, this underscores our recommendation that you minimize this type of approach, one that takes the process out of your control, and instead focus on contacting people you know or can get to know.

The Signature Line

After you have written your one- or two-paragraph closing, end your letter with what is called a "complimentary close." Two spaces below your last paragraph, type "Sincerely," "Sincerely yours," "Very truly yours," or another polite and customary phrase. Then space down three or four lines and type your name, exactly as it appears on the top of your resume and cover letter.

Two spaces below your name, add in a notation that indicates you have enclosed your resume. You can use "enclosure" or "attachment"—whichever you prefer.

If you are using a P.S., it should appear two spaces below the enclosure notation.

The Value of a P.S.

Think about letters that you have received that have included a P.S. (postscript). If you are like most readers, you immediately read the P.S., and then read it again after you read through the letter. With a P.S. you can close out your cover letter on a particularly powerful, positive note. Be sure your P.S. contains information that is of value to the employer. Here are two examples.

P.S. I was excited to learn about your planned distribution facility in Wilmington. When I opened a similar site for Custom Carriers, I built in technology and processes that made it the most efficient facility of more than 50 nationwide. I'd be happy to share these strategies with you during our meeting.

P.S. Congratulations on being named "Employer of the Year" for Essex County! I understand your employee retention has soared. I know some strategies that ensure that you are hiring (not just keeping) the best people—these strategies have proven to be successful in companies of all sizes. I will pass along my ideas when we meet.

Step 6: Proofread and Polish

Before sending your letter, it is important to make sure that it is error-free and reads well from start to finish. Carefully proofread your letter with attention to the following:

- **Spelling.** Begin by running your word processor's spell-check feature, but don't stop there! Read your letter slowly, word by word, to be sure that you haven't inadvertently typed "there" when you meant "their" or made some other spelling or word error that will not be caught by spell-check. Be extra certain that you have correctly spelled names, addresses, and company names. If you're not sure, make a phone call to find out.

- **Grammar and punctuation.** A grammatical error will create a poor impression. Make certain that you have correctly matched subjects with verbs, used appropriate punctuation, and used the right adjective and contraction for each instance.

- **Tone and flow.** Does your letter read well? Will the reader move smoothly from one paragraph to the next? Is the writing style consistent throughout? Is it polite, professional, respectful, and assertive but not aggressive?

If writing is not your strong suit, enlist the help of a friend or family member with excellent language skills. While this step should not take long, it is extremely important to take the time to polish your draft so that it clearly communicates your message to a potential employer in a positive and professional manner.

As soon as you complete your cover letter, take a few moments to copy the relevant parts to your worksheet or separate file. Keep a list of people you've written to, dates you've sent letters, follow-up timeline, and any outcomes.

> **Tip:** *We recommend that after you write your cover letters, you take a break, then come back for the proofreading and polishing step. You will find that this step goes more quickly and you are able to spot errors and improvements more easily.*

Job search requires you to organize and track a lot of material, and doing it a bit at a time is much more effective than ignoring these steps until you have a large pile to take care of.

Step 7: Choose the Transmission Method (Mail or E-mail)

As we have mentioned, you might be sending many of your cover letters by e-mail rather than printing the letters and sending them by postal mail, messenger, or hand delivery. While most of the steps will be the same, there are a few differences between the two transmission methods.

Printed Letters

Print your letter on good-quality bond paper that matches your resume. Double-check your print quality to be sure that the image is sharp, clear, and adequately dark. Custom-print an envelope to match.

Now, hand-sign your name in the space between the complimentary close and your typed name. Stack the cover letter on top of your resume, fold up one-third from the bottom and down one-third from the top, and insert your letter into the envelope.

If you prefer to mail your materials flat, place the cover letter on top of the resume and insert them unfolded into a 9 × 12 envelope. You can use a label to create the mailing address and return address (most printers can't accept 9 × 12 envelopes for direct printing).

E-mailed Letters

It is important that you take just as much care with an e-mail cover letter as you would with a printed letter. Don't let the informality of e-mail fool you into thinking it is not as important to tailor your message or proofread your document. It is! Be sure that you follow *every* step that we have explained above, except for the formatting guidelines.

We recommend that you create your e-mail messages separately in your word-processing file, then copy and paste them into the e-mail message area. This way you won't be tempted to skip the proofreading and spell-checking stages, and you'll find it easier to file and re-use your cover letters if you keep them in a separate documents file.

When sending an e-mail, it is not necessary to include the inside address (the name and address of the person you're writing to), nor do you have to type the date. Just start right in with your salutation ("Dear Ms. Anderson:"). Unless you are already on a first-name basis, we don't recommend that you use the person's first name or an informal greeting such as "Hey, Dennis." In many cases your e-mail message will be printed out and attached to your resume in the company files or shared with others in the company. It's important to establish the right tone, message, and impression.

The subject line of your e-mail message is important. It will help the recipient understand why you are writing (and thus keep your letter out of the spam file) and, later, can refresh his or her memory about who you are and what value you offer. Consider a subject line like one of these:

SUBJECT: Mtg. Mon. 11/22 – Jim Walker, Case Mgr.

SUBJECT: Jan Allen referral – Top sales rep (medical), Andy Smith

SUBJECT: Follow-up re: U.K. expansion, C. Jones

When sending a cover letter by e-mail, we recommend that you attach your resume as a Microsoft Word file. This is the format that is preferred by most recipients.

If you are not certain your recipient prefers a Word attachment, consider also including the text version of your resume in the body of your e-mail, below your cover letter. (In chapter 5, we provide instructions on how to create this format.) You might include a brief explanation below your signature: "My resume is attached in a Word file, but I have also pasted the text version below for your convenience."

Step 8: Send and Follow Up

Now it's time to hit "send," post your letter, arrange for delivery, or in some other way get it on its way to your recipient.

As soon as you send your letter, mark your calendar to follow up within the time frame you've specified. If you have not been specific, then mark your calendar for two days after an e-mail or hand delivery and four or five days after mailing a letter.

It is extremely important that you follow up! Otherwise, you will damage your credibility. Not only that, but following up while your material is fresh at hand will make the conversation more productive. Even employers who are anxious to hire find that their intended phone calls and interviews are often delayed because of the press of other priorities. Don't let your recipient forget about you—give them a call and ask if you can schedule a meeting. Keep your job search moving forward!

> **Tip:** *In formal and informal polls of hiring authorities, we have been told over and over how few people call to follow up after sending a cover letter and resume. Most people just don't do it. Making this kind of call can be intimidating— you feel like your career is on the line— and it's natural to avoid things we don't like. But we urge you to overcome these concerns and pick up the phone. You will make better progress in your job search, and you will immediately set yourself apart from the vast majority of job seekers who do not take this initiative.*

Key Points: Chapter 2

Follow these eight simple steps to create and send cover letters quickly and efficiently:

- **Step 1: Create Your Format:** Design a page layout that you can use for all of your job-search correspondence. Keep it simple, easy to create, easy to read, and coordinated with your resume.

- **Step 2: Add the Basics:** Start each letter with a date, inside address, and salutation. Double-check all names and spelling.

- **Step 3: State Why You're Writing and Get the Reader's Attention:** Refer immediately to your upcoming meeting or referral source. If you haven't been able to make contact before sending your letter, create a brief, interesting opening that will make your reader want to learn more.

- **Step 4: Share Information Relevant to the Reader's Needs:** This is the most important part of your cover letter. You must provide specific examples from your experience that are relevant to the needs and concerns of your recipient. Create a library of items from this section so that you can quickly pick-and-choose those that are right for a specific letter. Edit and customize to be sure you are addressing the needs you have uncovered.

- **Step 5: Close with an Action Statement:** Don't leave the ball in the employer's court! Be polite and positive yet assertive in your closing. Let the employer know that you want further dialogue and that you will follow up.

- **Step 6: Proofread and Polish:** Be certain that each cover letter is error-free, looks good, and reads smoothly from start to finish.

- **Step 7: Choose the Transmission Method** (Mail or E-mail): Follow the final steps to get your letter from your computer to your recipient. Print and mail, or paste and e-mail. Pay attention to details such as signing your name (in a paper letter) and creating a relevant subject line (for an e-mail message).

- **Step 8: Send and Follow Up:** Send your letter and immediately schedule your next step; then be sure that you follow up professionally and promptly, as promised.

Chapter 3

A Stupendous Collection of Professionally Written and Designed Cover Letters

This chapter presents 34 cover letters in a variety of styles and for a variety of professions. While we don't suggest you "copy" the content of any of these samples, they provide good ideas on how others have handled opening language, format, closing paragraphs, and overall tone and flow. Review the sample letters to find ideas on how to design and write your own cover letters. In most cases, you will see that the candidates have taken the initiative to call and perhaps even set up a meeting ahead of time, but in a few instances they have not been able to do so and are sending "cold" letters. For each letter we have identified the situation and added a few comments about the content, style, format, or circumstances of that particular letter.

Letter 1: Pre-Interview, for a Specific Job Opening

Comments: In his letter, Matt conveys both the hard skills and the intangibles that make him a great mechanic.

Matt Young   249 Maple Grove Road ▪ East Haven, CT 06512 ▪ 203-467-1276

March 15, 2005

Stanley Cohen
President
Savin Industrial
2590 East Haven Parkway
New Haven, CT 06510

Dear Mr. Cohen:

Thanks for taking my call and discussing your available mechanic position. I am very interested.

People say that I can fix anything. While that might not be true, I do have a wide range of skills and experience that can help keep your equipment and your facility running smoothly and safely.

I have spent my career building, fixing, and maintaining equipment for manufacturing and construction companies. I have a strong natural mechanical aptitude and the resourcefulness to solve any number of equipment problems, and I have continuously added to my skills through training, team projects, and the willingness to tackle just about anything.

The enclosed resume describes the breadth of my experience, but it cannot convey the creativity and energy I bring to every job nor the satisfaction I get from making machinery and equipment run well.

I look forward to our interview at 8:30 a.m. on the 8th. It will be a pleasure to meet you.

Sincerely,

Matt Young

enclosure: resume

Letter 2: No Interview Is Scheduled

Comments: Dion heads up this letter with a quote directly from a recent magazine interview with Mr. Sanderson. Later in the letter he refers to his phone call and mentions Mr. Sanderson's assistant by name.

Dion Maxwell

119 Old Possum Way, Middlefield, CT 06455 — 860-247-0904 — dionmaxwell@hotmail.com

---

March 15, 2005

Mr. Curtis Sanderson
President, Oxbow Industries
25 Main Street
Middletown, CT 06457

Dear Mr. Sanderson:

"We're always looking for employees who have a good attitude and a great work ethic." —*Curtis Sanderson,* Connecticut Business Journal *2/25/05*

When I read this quote from your recent interview, I knew that I had what you are looking for—the qualities you seek in your best employees, plus skills that are a great fit for your growing Middletown distribution center.

I have more than 20 years of experience at a small milling plant where I filled a variety of roles—changing job duties and pitching in where needed to keep our products moving out the door. I am a licensed forklift operator, capable machinery operator, experienced shift supervisor, and leader in the areas of quality and safety. My work ethic and reliability are second to none.

When I spoke with Adelyn in your office this week, she suggested that I forward my resume directly to your attention. I will call again in a few days to determine the next steps. Thank you for your consideration.

Sincerely,

Dion Maxwell

enclosure

Letter 3: No Interview Is Scheduled

Comments: Not able to connect via phone, Jack sends his resume and references both his phone call and his referral source. He shows he is knowledgeable about new challenges the company is facing and relates how his skills and experience can be of value.

Jack Wallace

2459 Arroyo Drive, Louisville, CO 80027 ▪ (303) 761-8710 ▪ jackwallace@gmail.com

Electronic Prepress Production & Project Management

March 15, 2005

Janice Rodriguez
Vice President of Marketing
Denver Graphics, Inc.
794 Silver Street
Denver, CO 80020

Dear Ms. Rodriguez:

Following up on the phone message I left you last week, I am forwarding my resume at the suggestion of Tom Anders, who was my manager at Mountain Prepress before he joined your company as production manager of your Boulder facility.

Tom thought that you would be interested in my 10 years of experience in all facets of electronic prepress, project management, and graphic design, especially as you ramp up to support the printing and publishing needs for XYZ Corp.'s newly relocated headquarters.

Highlights of my qualifications include the following:

- Eleven years in electronic prepress production for high-end commercial printers
- Experience with both Macintosh and Windows systems and a record of leadership in integrating Mac systems into traditional high-end production processes
- Expert knowledge of industry-standard software including QuarkXPress, Photoshop, ArtPro, Illustrator, PageMaker, and FreeHand; plus additional knowledge of business software (MS Office Suite) and network computer operations
- Education in commercial art; graphic design skills as evidenced through successful freelance work

My recent work in network support has broadened my capabilities in all areas of computer operations, yet I am eager to return to a dedicated prepress/project management/design role where my strongest talents can benefit both the company and its customers.

May we meet to explore your needs and the value I offer your company? I will call within the next few days in hopes of setting up a meeting. Thank you.

Sincerely,

Jack Wallace

enclosure: resume

Letter 4: No Interview Is Scheduled

Comments: Diane was unable to find out more about the company or the opportunity because this was a "blind" ad. However, she knew that it was in the real-estate management industry, so she highlighted her strong, relevant experience in her cover letter.

Diane Sanborn

402-209-3409 ■ sanborn_d@hotmail.com
6753 Village Circle #5B, Omaha, NE 68125

March 15, 2005

News Box 759-B
Omaha News-Record
2525 Elm Street
Omaha, NE 68101

Re: Administrative Assistant — Real Estate Management Company

Your current opening sounds tailor-made for my experience in challenging administrative/accounting roles with ABC Properties. Managing diverse projects and functions in a fast-paced environment, I helped the company increase its revenue and profits while better serving its tenants. For example —

- Our monthly rental accounting/deposit process was taking more than two full weeks due to the thousands of units we managed and an inefficient method for collecting and tracking payments. I was able to cut that time in half while also eliminating risky cash payments and better utilizing our on-site staff.

- Recognizing the need for faster and more expert response to inquiries from tenants and leasing staff, I helped create the position of Senior Administrative Assistant and became the front-line responder for all calls and inquiries. This improved tenant satisfaction and gave our leasing staff faster, more accurate information.

Having handled a high volume of detailed reporting and accounting activities, I am accustomed to a fast pace and a diverse workload. I am very familiar with tenant issues, leasing questions, and the specialized software used for property management. And I have a history of showing initiative, taking on new projects, and exercising good judgment in daily decision-making.

I would like to learn more about your current position. I am confident my skills and experience will enable me to make immediate contributions to the success of your company.

Sincerely,

Diane Sanborn

attachment: resume

■ ■ ■

Letter 5: No Interview Is Scheduled

Comments: Cecilia opens her letter by mentioning the name of her referral source. This technique gets the reader's attention and gives Cecilia added credibility.

Cecilia Evans, Ph.D.
Pianist, Composer, Teacher
4509 Prairie Street ▪ Omaha, NE 68106 ▪ 402-349-1249 ▪ cevans@aol.com

---

March 15, 2005

Sandra Lee, Executive Director
Omaha Symphony & Pops Orchestra
119 East Church Street
Omaha, NE 68109

Dear Ms. Lee:

At the suggestion of Dina Whitman, I am contacting you to express my interest in the open position of Principal Pianist with the Omaha Pops.

With more than 20 years of professional experience as a pianist, accompanist, composer, and music teacher, I offer strong qualifications:

- Master's degree in piano performance and Ph.D. in music composition.
- Orchestral and chamber music performance experience (including extensive soloist experience) in the U.S., England, Ireland, and Holland, performing a wide array of classical and popular programs.
- Vast repertoire of both classical and nonclassical music including Broadway and jazz pieces.
- Broad experience as an accompanist and music director for dance, theater, and opera.

After reviewing the enclosed resume and visiting with me, I think you will agree that I have the professional skills, work ethic, musicianship, and teamwork attitude that will make me a successful addition to your orchestra. I look forward to meeting with you and Maestro Schwinn; I will call early next week to schedule an appointment at a time that is convenient for you both.

Thank you for your consideration.

Sincerely,

Cecilia Evans, Ph.D.

enclosure

Letter 6: No Interview Is Scheduled

Comments: Trying to break into the competitive field of pharmaceutical sales, Jamie has "gone to school" with an existing rep for the company and learned a lot about the profession. The cover letter is full of very specific sales-related achievements.

Jamie Van Horn

253 Silverton Trail, Phoenix, AZ 85017
602-779-1682 • jvanhorn@yahoo.com

March 15, 2005

Sally Osborne
Southwest District Manager
Pfizer Pharmaceuticals
6512 Scottsdale Boulevard
Phoenix, AZ 85010

Dear Ms. Osborne:

Sandra Lopez has suggested I forward my resume to you for consideration for a current sales opening in the Southwest District of Pfizer Pharmaceuticals.

Through conversations and ride-alongs with Sandra, I have learned what it takes to be a successful pharmaceutical sales representative, and I am confident I have the drive, dedication, and proven skills that will enable me to quickly become productive. Highlights of my career experiences include

- **Consistent performance above goals in direct-sales positions:**
  - **130%, 2002–2003**
  - **115%, 2001–2002**
  - **141%, 2000–2001**
- **Trend of sales growth in competitive environments:**
  - **25%, 15%, and 6% growth in diverse sales departments, 1997–2000**
  - **10% growth as a result of community marketing and visibility/ awareness campaigns, 2003–present**
- **25% year-over-year sales increase as sales manager**
- **Initiative and leadership in developing relationship-marketing programs**
- **Management experience and proven strengths in organization, planning, and follow-through**

I would like to meet with you to explore how my background and talents can benefit your company as a sales representative in the Greater Phoenix area, and I will call within a few days to get your thoughts and possibly schedule a meeting. Thank you.

Sincerely,

Jamie Van Horn

attachment: resume

Letter 7: Pre-Interview, for a Specific Job Opening

Comments: A meeting has been set, and the cover letter and resume are sent to reinforce this candidate's expertise and highly relevant achievements.

Anthony Andretti

25 Elm Street, Ridgefield, CT 06877 ■ Home 203-455-1265 ■ Mobile 203-421-8712 ■ a-andretti@verizon.net

---

March 15, 2005

Michaela Standish
President
Apex Products, Inc.
759 Madison Avenue
New York, NY 10020

Dear Ms. Standish:

In advance of our meeting next Tuesday at 10:00, I am sending along some background material, as you suggested. I am excited about the opportunity to expand Apex into Europe, and—as you will see in the attached—I have deep experience and a strong track record of success in that region.

For more than 10 years I have achieved profitable sales growth for companies in the U.S., Europe, and Asia. This multinational experience has given me a deep understanding of how to sell within each country's unique culture, and I am expert in creating strategic sales plans that achieve niche market penetration, dramatic revenue growth, and successful entry into new markets.

These brief highlights of my experience indicate my ability to deliver bottom-line benefits:

- As Senior Sales Executive for Master Microchips, I developed $5 million in first-year sales during the company's first expansion into international markets.

- As International Sales Manager for Tech-Line, I spearheaded new-product sales worldwide including a heavy presence in Europe. Capturing business with major OEMs was a key factor in the highly successful launch of our new product.

- For a technology start-up in Germany, I created and executed a strategic plan that resulted in successful penetration into a niche market—averaging 63% annual growth during my tenure.

- Consistently, I formed beneficial strategic alliances with customers and suppliers, developing partnership models that resulted in rapid business growth—e.g., growing Tech-Line from start-up to $2 million revenue in 6 months, and then quadrupling to $8 million in just over 2 years.

As an accomplished sales and marketing executive, I know how to lead international efforts to meet revenue objectives and market-penetration goals. I am confident I can achieve growth objectives for Apex in Europe, and at our meeting I look forward to exploring the challenges and opportunities in more detail.

Sincerely,

Anthony Andretti

enclosure: resume

Letter 8: No Interview Is Scheduled

Comments: This new college graduate is assertively pursuing a position in pharmaceutical sales. His letter (shown in e-mail format) follows up on an earlier conversation and makes the case for an interview.

SUBJECT: Follow-up to discussion re: pharm. sales

Dear Ms. Andreatti:

Thank you for taking the time to speak with me about careers in pharmaceutical sales. Since our discussion, I have been reading and learning more about the field, and from what I have learned, Pharmedix is the right company and sales is the right profession for me!

Throughout my college career and employment experience, I have consistently thrived in demanding and results-focused assignments, proving that I can bring the following qualities to Pharmedix:

== **Outstanding leadership and communication skills,** demonstrated in diverse roles where I have shown the ability to contribute, motivate, inspire, and build consensus.

== **Sales and customer focus,** repeatedly proven in challenging business environments. I have participated in the sales process, prepared presentations, responded to customer inquiries and problems, and developed programs to meet the needs of customers and constituents.

== **Educational achievement.** I am about to graduate from the University of Virginia with a 3.43 GPA and a BS degree in Business and a minor in Biology. In leadership roles with several organizations, I have directed very successful campus-wide programs, led teams, and built support for new ideas.

I hope you will agree that I can be successful in a sales role for your company. I will call you next week to see whether we can schedule a time to meet.

Again, thank you for your support and assistance.

Sincerely,

Troy Harris

****
My resume is attached as a Word file, and a text version is also pasted below for your convenience.

Letter 9: Pre-Interview, for a Specific Job Opening

Comments: David has set up a meeting with the regional sales manager for a sports-related product company. In his letter he highlights his relevant experience and success. In the closing paragraph, he hints at some good ideas that can help the company.

David Adams
deeadams@hotmail.com

2349 Bishop St., #4A, Valley Glen, CA 91405
Home 818-978-0904 ■ Mobile 818-203-0090

March 15, 2005

Mr. James Lee
Sales Director, Western Region
Fourth Down Products
2529 Alameda Avenue
Los Angeles, CA 90045

Dear Mr. Lee:

Thank you for agreeing to meet with me next Wednesday. Based on our initial conversation, it seems that my ability to sell "solutions" rather than products is a good fit for your needs as you seek to expand your visibility in the Western U.S.

As noted in the enclosed resume, I have led an under-performing product division from "bit player" to its current performance: generating 33% of total revenue (up from 5%) at our location, and delivering, from a single location, 25% of total sales for our 20-site company.

Having completed this turnaround over the last 5 years, I'm eager for new challenges where my proven skills in sales, marketing, and program/event planning can contribute to a company's bottom line.

I have been thinking about the challenges you described in building your presence at the retail level, and I have some good ideas to share at our meeting. I'm excited about the future of Fourth Down and eager to contribute to your growth.

Sincerely,

David Adams

enclosure

Letter 10: No Interview Is Scheduled

Comments: Talia builds upon a chance encounter at a breakfast meeting and follows up with this executive to try to land an interview for a specific job opening.

Talia T. Zinn
795 Chesapeake Drive
302-349-1245   Wilmington, DE 19805   ttzinn@hotmail.com

March 30, 2005

William Howe
Regional Manager
Shoppers' World
25 Victory Parkway
Wilmington, DE 19801

Dear Mr. Howe:

I enjoyed speaking with you at the Chamber breakfast today and was very interested to learn of your pending managerial opening. As you suggested, I am following up with a resume.

As a successful manager for a fast-growing specialty retailer, operating three locations with distinct marketing, inventory, and customer-relations needs, I repeatedly proved my ability to deliver results, including

- profitable sales growth
- rejuvenated customer loyalty
- effective merchandising and smart product selection
- community presence and positive image-building

I have successfully tackled the challenges of store start-up, new niche-market entry, and performance turnaround. In every location I have built loyal, dedicated, hard-working teams that share my passion for customer service and retail excellence.

After many years in the Pacific Northwest, I recently returned to the Wilmington area to be closer to my aging parents. I was intrigued to see how quickly Shoppers' World has grown in this area, and I'm eager to contribute to that growth.

I will call in a day or two in hopes of setting a meeting.

Sincerely,

Talia T. Zinn

enclosure: resume

Letter 11: No Interview Is Scheduled

Comments: Ellen is seeking to make a career change from corporate marketing to a university setting. She carefully correlates her experience to the needs of the college.

ELLEN SWANSON

203-484-7948   25 Woodwind Drive, Northford, CT 06472   eswanson@yahoo.com

March 15, 2005

Steven Rogoff, Ed.D.
Vice President
Clinton College
259 Eli Drive
North Haven, CT 06473

Dear Dr. Rogoff:

My neighbor, Clyde Stanton, has told me that you are looking for a new Director of Development for Clinton College. As a follow-up to the voice-mail message I left you last week, I am contacting you to express my interest in this position and share some indication of the value I offer.

My track record in corporate marketing and sales provides the foundation for success as your Director of Development. Whether positioning products or less tangible items such as a liberal arts education, it is essential to package and present solutions that meet consumers' needs, stir their interest, and communicate a strong brand message. I am a keen advocate of liberal arts education, having graduated from Smith College, and understand its value in today's complex business environment and global economy.

These achievements are representative of the value I can bring to the college:

- Heading a company's first formal product-development function, I launched a strategically focused and aggressive development program that resulted in products that now represent more than 50% of company revenue. *Value to Clinton: bringing the right ideas to the development program at the right time and with the right message; succeeding in intensely competitive market conditions.*

- Given a turnaround challenge, I led the division to sustained growth and returned it to profitability. *Value to Clinton: continuing Clinton's recent fundraising successes and building on these accomplishments; focusing efforts on strategic priorities; energizing and leading a team to outperform expectations.*

- In a direct-sales role, I achieved sales two to three times greater than my peers. *Value to Clinton: using proven sales, communication, and relationship-building skills to achieve rapid results.*

I know you will be reviewing candidates who have lengthy experience in academic environments. Please consider my strong business background as added value, combining proven management, sales, and marketing skills with a deep commitment to liberal arts education.

Thank you for your consideration. I will call you next week to answer any questions you might have and see whether we can schedule an appointment.

Sincerely,

Ellen Swanson

enclosure: resume

Letter 12: No Interview Is Scheduled

Comments: This letter responds to a blind ad and briefly highlights excellent experience that is directly related to the position.

TRICIA BILLINGS
London, England (through July 2005)
TriciaBillings@msn.com

March 15, 2005

Re: Market Development Manager: Posting #794-MDM

Your advertised opening for a Market Development Manager describes interesting challenges. My background and accomplishments seem to be a good match for your needs, and I'd like to explore this opportunity with you.

For 18 years I have delivered strong business results for company operations in Europe and the U.S. Most recently, I took on the challenge of rapidly growing Standard Tool's business in the U.K. In two years, we increased sales nearly four-fold through highly effective market-entry strategies, brand repositioning, and organizational restructuring.

Previously, with Global Supplies, I was instrumental in successful market entry into Western and Eastern Europe, with results that outperformed goals for both sales and profits.

May we schedule a time to talk? I am always accessible via e-mail and can arrange a phone call immediately or an in-person visit during one of my frequent trips to the U.S.

Thank you.

Sincerely,

Tricia Billings

enclosure: resume

Letter 13: Interview Is Scheduled, No Specific Job Opening

Comments: Notice how Sylvia immediately informs Mr. Barnes that she has already followed up on a lead he gave her during their phone conversation. This shows that she has initiative and good follow-through skills.

Sylvia Brock
203-484-1287

94 Old River Road
Northford, CT 06472
sylvia_brock@snet.net

March 30, 2005

Alan Barnes
Vice President, Sales & Operations
Micro-Solution Company
245 Peabody Street
Hamden, CT 06517

Dear Mr. Barnes:

I am so glad that I called you this morning, and I do appreciate your very helpful ideas. I have a call in to John McManus and will let you know how that goes; and I am pleased to send along my resume in advance of our meeting next week.

As I mentioned, my background includes high-level customer and account management experience as well as complex project management responsibilities. My eight years of professional experience have taught me that my talents and expertise are best suited to a role that involves sales, heavy customer interaction, multiple task management, and high performance expectations.

Your company's products, reputation, and growth potential are exciting. I believe my skills will be a good fit for your needs as you expand, and I look forward to exploring this in more detail when we meet.

Sincerely,

Sylvia Brock

enclosure

Letter 14: No Interview Is Scheduled

Comments: In this T-style letter (written in response to a blind ad), notice how Joshua supplies everything the employer is looking for—and more. As we noted in chapter 2, however, this kind of letter is not effective unless you are a perfect match for every qualification requested.

Joshua Trent
joshuatrent@verizon.net

4525 Parkview Crescent
Indianapolis, IN 46218
317-454-2094

March 15, 2005

P.O. Box 4592
Indianapolis, IN 46201-4592

Re: **Corporate Communications Staff Writer**

My skills and experience are an excellent match for your requirements for a Staff Writer:

Your Requirements	**My Experience, Skills, and Value Offered**
2 years' business writing experience	**Four years' experience creating diverse business messages,** from corporate communications to feature articles and radio broadcast material.
Ability to complete projects on deadline	**Proven project coordination skills and tight deadline focus.** My current role as producer of a daily 3-hour talk-radio program requires planning, coordination, and execution of many detailed tasks, always in the face of inflexible deadlines.
Oral presentation skills................,......	**Unusually broad experience,** including high-profile roles as an on-air radio presence and "the voice" for an on-hold telephone message company.
Relevant education (BA or BS)	**BA** in Mass Communications; 1 year post-graduate study in Multimedia Communications.

As you will note from the enclosed resume, my experience encompasses corporate, print media, and multimedia environments. I offer a diverse and proven skill set that can help your company create and deliver its message to various audiences to build image, market presence, and revenue.

May we meet to explore the value I offer your company as its next Staff Writer?

Sincerely,

Joshua Trent

enclosure: resume

Letter 15: Pre-Interview, for a Specific Job Opening

Comments: Dale called to find out more about the position before sending a letter and resume. Her effort paid off! In addition to citing relevant achievements, she includes a "teaser" in the last paragraph that communicates she is already hard at work for what she hopes will be her new company.

Subject: Prep for our mtg on 4/5 re: Acct Exec position

Dear Ms. Anthony:

Thank you for the information you shared with regard to your Account Executive position. Your need to create quick growth for your new .Net publication is a great fit for my experience at Smythe Publications.

As Regional and National Sales Manager with Smythe, I have delivered results for every one of my multiple publications serving various audiences in the high-tech market:

- For our flagship publication, C++ Calling, I elevated sales 339% in the challenging 2003–2004 market.
- Taking over two niche publications, I quickly generated new revenue from key target accounts including Sun and Dell.
- Handed a "dying" publication, I doubled ad sales in five months and grew the business so much that three new staff were added to handle the volume.
- For Joe Java Journal, in my first high-tech publishing assignment, I became the top salesperson and increased revenue 77% in 6 months.

In brief, I am a highly accomplished sales professional who gets results by listening to my customers and developing creative solutions that meet their needs. (I have the highest account retention rate at my company.) My background in selling diverse products and services gives me an exceptionally strong base in sales fundamentals, and I am driven to set and exceed aggressive goals.

I have been thinking about some ways to achieve a quick growth spurt in the emerging .Net marketplace, and I look forward to sharing these with you at our meeting at 10:30 on April 5. If you have any questions before then, you can always reach me at my mobile number, 415-292-1276.

Best regards,

Dale Gelman

****
My resume is attached as a Word file and is also pasted below in text format for your convenience.

Letter 16: Pre-Interview, No Specific Job Opening

Comments: A chance meeting at a business function led to this follow-up letter. The headline (carried over from his resume) emphasizes Daniel's specific experience in health care, and all of his qualifications and achievements are directly relevant to the needs of his audience.

DANIEL T. SILVER

203-484-2165   394 Beech Street, North Branford, CT 06471   dsilver@msn.com

CONSTRUCTION PROJECT MANAGER

Healthcare Facilities • Medical Equipment Installations • Special-Purpose Facilities

March 15, 2005

Alex DaSilva
Vice President, Facilities
Nutmeg Healthcare, Inc.
171 Whalley Avenue
New Haven, CT 06510

Dear Alex:

I enjoyed our conversation at the Chamber of Commerce Expo and, as you suggested, am following up to share some additional information prior to getting together.

With extensive experience managing healthcare construction projects, I can bring valuable expertise to Nutmeg. My qualifications include both formal training (B.S. in Construction Management) and more than 15 years of construction experience. For the last five years, I have managed diverse projects within the ConnHealth organization, including the following:

- Complete renovation of Middletown Hospital to an administrative facility.
- Medical equipment installations (e.g., 4 Cath Labs) requiring pinpoint precision in scheduling and managing multiple contractors on a tight schedule.
- Patient floor renovation to a decentralized nursing model and to include holistic features such as sculpture, stained glass, and audio elements.

As a project manager, in addition to strong planning, organizational, communication, and leadership skills, I am a good in-field decision-maker and have frequently been able to save money, save time, and eliminate inefficiencies by coming up with practical and creative solutions to the questions and challenges that invariably arise on the site. I maintain excellent relationships with subcontractors and vendors.

In a nutshell, I am committed to meeting deadlines and budgets and delivering the best possible results to my customer. I would like to explore how I can deliver this value to Nutmeg, and I will call within a few days to schedule our meeting at a time that is convenient to you.

Sincerely yours,

Daniel T. Silver

enclosure

Letter 17: No Interview Is Scheduled

Comments: Tina contacted Dr. Rodriguez by phone but was unable to secure an appointment right away. She states exactly when she will call to follow up.

Tina McIntosh

Home 512-654-1276 • Office 512-984-4050
7945 Corrales Trail, Austin, TX 78745

March 15, 2005

Robert Rodriguez
Superintendent of School
Round Rock School District
1597 School Street
Round Rock, TX 78681

Dear Dr. Rodriguez:

I appreciate your taking the time to talk with me on Wednesday. As you suggested, I am following up with additional details of my background and credentials.

My philosophy is that strong educational performance begins with the fundamentals: student participation, teacher engagement, safe schools, and clear expectations from administrators and parents. Beginning with these fundamentals and building strong programs and policies to establish them, I have delivered a remarkable turnaround as principal of South Fork High School:

- From "academic emergency" to meeting 100% of standards on the building report card.
- From 75% graduation rate to 86%.
- From sub-par attendance to the highest in our county.

As a result, we are attracting attention and drawing more students than ever from our open-enrollment district.

From our conversation, it seems that your challenges in Round Rock require just the leadership and experience I have to offer. I am eager to prove my ability to improve performance, create cultural change, and deliver results in your district.

I will call you on Friday to follow up, and I hope we can meet soon.

Sincerely,

Tina McIntosh

Enclosure: resume

Letter 18: No Interview Is Scheduled

Comments: This letter contains quite a bit of personal information because it helps to explain Danielle's motivation for becoming a cooking instructor.

Danielle Prince
45 Bayview Road, East Providence, RI 02915
401-909-1254 • dani@ri.rr.com

March 15, 2005

Philip Swansea
Executive Director
Rhode Island Culinary Institute
294 Roger Williams Boulevard
Providence, RI 02909

Dear Chef Swansea:

Thank you for taking the time to speak with me recently. As promised, I am sending you my resume in advance of further discussions.

I would like to tell you a little bit about myself that is not included in my resume. I have had a love of food and cooking since I was about nine and my mother bought me a cookbook called "Around the World Cooking for Children." With my first French meal, I thought I was on my way to a career in food service.

This goal was sidetracked for about a year in college, where I studied Elementary Education. After missing my passion, I decided to go to Johnson & Wales Culinary School to pursue a degree. As I got older, I realized I could combine both passions—cooking and education—and have the best of both worlds.

Over the years I have taught cooking classes for both adults and children. Now I'd like to take it one step further. A part-time position that could lead to more involvement would be ideal.

I've heard such positive feedback about you and your chef education program. I would love the chance to meet with you and see if there is an opportunity for me in your program.

I will follow up with a phone call next week.

Thank you!

Danielle Prince

enclosure

Letter 19: Pre-Interview, for a Specific Job Opening

Comments: Sam, a veterinarian, was relocating. He planned a visit and called ahead to set up this meeting with a veterinary practice in his new location.

Sam Granada, DVM

7949 42nd Avenue SW, Seattle, WA 98136
samgee@aol.com • 202-239-6543

March 15, 2005

Edward Kozak, DVM
Montgomery Animal Clinic
10449 Montgomery Road
Cincinnati, OH 45242

Dear Dr. Kozak:

Thank you for agreeing to meet with me during my visit to Cincinnati next week. I look forward to speaking with you about the new associate position with your clinic and how my blend of qualifications and capabilities can benefit your patients, your clients, your team, and your practice.

I have had a satisfying ten-year career as an associate with a thriving practice outside Seattle. As small-animal practitioners in a rural area, we see a diverse caseload, perform surgery daily at our facility, and work collaboratively with veterinary specialists for complex cases. I have built excellent relationships with our clients while caring for their pets.

Because I will be relocating to my hometown of Cincinnati in the next several months, I am seeking a new veterinarian position. It sounds like your clinic has a great mix of small-animal cases that would be a good fit for my skills—I look forward to learning more next week!

If you have any questions in the meantime, please feel free to call me at my home number (above) until the 18th; in Cincinnati I can be reached at 513-791-7632.

Sincerely,

Sam Granada, DVM

enclosure—resume

Letter 20: No Interview Is Scheduled

Comments: This e-mail cover letter is brief but includes a lot of valuable information.

Dear Ms. Gold:

My sister, Tracy Oswald, tells me that you are looking for a systems administrator for your growing San Francisco operation.

I am experienced, reliable, loyal, and customer focused and would like to talk with you about joining your team.

The enclosed resume describes nearly 15 years of experience with Anthem Blue Cross/Blue Shield, during which I advanced to increasingly responsible technical positions. Whether working independently or with a team, I worked hard to provide the best possible service and support to my "customers." I was recognized for my strong technical skills, ability to guide less experienced support people, and 100% reliability.

A recent downsizing at Anthem caused my position to be eliminated, and I am looking for a new opportunity with a company like yours, where my technical abilities, positive attitude, and dedication will be valued.

I will call you next week in hopes of getting together soon.

Yours truly,

Kevin Oswald

****
My resume is attached as a Word document and also pasted below in text format for your convenience.

Letter 21: Pre-Interview, for a Specific Job Opening

Comments: This letter hits on the high points that will be of most interest to the target company, a provider of technology project management services to large corporations.

Maria Dunham
1749 Calumet Farm Drive, Loveland, OH 45140
H: 513-742-1745 — M: 513-249-1265 — mdunham@cinci.rr.com

March 15, 2005

Vijay Krishnan
Redhawk Technology Consultants
75 Edwin Moses Boulevard, Suite C
Dayton, OH 45440

Dear Mr. Krishnan:

The technical and project management opportunities at Redhawk are exciting, and I am looking forward to following up our recent phone conversation with a more in-depth discussion. Prior to our meeting at 3 p.m. next Wednesday, I am forwarding some information on how I can help your company and its clients.

Relevant to the needs you shared, I offer technical strengths and a strong background in project leadership. Currently, as the sole project manager within Midwest Bank's Electronic Forms Unit, I direct technology projects from needs assessment and technical-requirement writing through implementation, user training, and documentation. Working collaboratively with diverse project teams—made up of both technical professionals from the different business units and non-technical end-users—I guide the people and oversee the project to ensure business goals are met.

Business benefits from projects under my leadership include millions of dollars in cost savings and significant reductions in labor-intensive tasks, thus freeing staff for more productive and more stimulating work.

I am accustomed to a fast-paced environment and to overseeing multiple simultaneous projects.

If you have any questions prior to our meeting, please don't hesitate to call; I am most accessible via my mobile phone, 513-249-1265.

Sincerely,

Maria Dunham

enclosure: resume

Letter 22: Pre-Interview, No Specific Job Opening

Comments: This letter makes a convincing case for a career change. It is written as a follow-up to a phone call to a network contact.

Natasha Sturtz   7141 Jonquil Lane, Cincinnati, OH 45241 • 513-218-3076 • sturtz@gmail.com

---

March 15, 2005

Mr. David Tallant
Chief Information Officer
COM-TECH
2525 Technology Parkway
Cincinnati, OH 45207

Dear Mr. Tallant:

I look forward to meeting with you next week—John has told me so many interesting things about you, it will be a pleasure to meet you in person! Before our meeting, I am providing my resume, as you requested, and a bit of background that explains my current career direction.

Since 2002, I have completed my MCSE, MCP+I, and A+ certifications and am well on my way to completing the Windows Server 2003 component of the MCSE.

What sets me apart from others who may have similar qualifications is my record of thriving in extremely challenging work environments, quickly learning new skills, and demonstrating a passion for excellence.

My background in the highly demanding restaurant industry gives me an edge in any work environment. In that competitive, high-pressure field, I consistently performed to high standards and was singled out for prestigious opportunities.

Now, I am very interested in pursuing a position in line with my recent education. I offer more than just core technical abilities. I have worked in management for many years, and although a position in management may not be what you have available, you will find that I bring to your company a higher level of maturity and responsibility than most. I am dedicated and punctual, have a powerful work ethic, and enjoy new challenges.

If given an opportunity with your company, I am confident I will continue my record of thriving and contributing in every new situation. Thank you for agreeing to meet with me; I look forward to exploring your needs and any solutions I can offer.

Sincerely,

Natasha Sturtz

enclosure

Letter 23: Pre-Interview, for a Specific Job Opening

Comments: This T-style letter is used to show how this candidate exceeds all of the job requirements.

Jon Lee Novak
11 White Oak Lane, Laconia, NH 03246
603-349-1256 • jlnovak@gmail.com

March 15, 2005

Tom Hennessey
Northeast Logistics
19 Apple Street
Reading, MA 01867

Dear Mr. Hennessey:

I appreciate the information you shared with me on the phone today with regard to your Logistics Engineer opening. As you suggested, I am forwarding my resume for your review before we meet.

Relevant to your needs, I offer engineering expertise, logistics experience, and a track record of measurable contributions to operational effectiveness:

Your Requirements	*My Qualifications*
Bachelor's degree or 3 years' experience in warehousing/logistics	• BS Mechanical Engineering • More than 10 years' experience in logistics, operations, and engineering project management in fast-paced distribution settings
Operational and data analysis, problem definition, solution development	History of developing innovative and *effective* solutions to diverse operational challenges: • Root cause analysis • Technology and process implementation • Project planning and management • Facilities and logistics systems design
Report and data development	Proven ability to define and produce meaningful data for business decision-making: • Created new productivity and quality reporting using data from a new warehouse management system. • Developed data that pointed to root cause of inventory control problems, then put in place a program that quickly improved service levels by more than 5%.
Project management	An unbroken record of delivering projects on schedule and on/under budget.

Mr. Hennessey, I look forward to meeting you at 11:30 on Friday.

Sincerely,

Jon Lee Novak

Attachment: Resume

Letter 24: Pre-Interview, No Specific Job Opening

Comments: This format is a clever way to call attention to qualifications in three distinct areas.

Stephen Francis

2940 Sweet Rose Drive, Dunwoody, GA 30338
Home 678-290-3409 ▪ Mobile 678-987-1256 ▪ sfrancis@yahoo.com

March 30, 2005

Ms. Edwina Forrest
Vice President of Engineering
Schwartz Precision Tools
909 Peachtree Boulevard Extension
Atlanta, GA 30303

Dear Ms. Forrest:

Thank you for your time on the phone today. I am excited about exploring opportunities with Schwarz Precision Tools at our meeting next week.

My qualifications encompass the following:

Expertise	▪ Master's degree in Mechanical Engineering. ▪ International project experience (U.S., South America, Europe) with two leading German companies providing engineering, automation, and plant design in the mining and cement industries. ▪ Two successful patent applications and a background in industrial R&D.
Relationships	▪ History of restoring customer confidence through creative solutions that overcome obstacles and deliver customer benefits. ▪ Effective communication skills across multicultural environments with clients, colleagues, and senior management.
Results	▪ Record of key contributions to multimillion-dollar plant engineering projects including saving corporate profits, cutting customer downtime, establishing best practices, and developing new engineering applications. ▪ Leadership of successful market-entry engineering and project initiatives.

I have long been impressed with your company's technical expertise and ability to expand into new markets. I'd like to add to your success and look forward to exploring some possibilities. I will see you at 3 pm on the 5th.

Sincerely yours,

Stephen Francis

enclosure: resume

Letter 25: No Interview Is Scheduled

Comments: Written to a network contact, this letter and the accompanying resume set the stage for an interview.

Amanda Klein

4509 Charlfont Street, Cincinnati, OH 45249
513-891-3651   amanda_klein@cinci.rr.com

March 30, 2005

Mr. Chris Welles
Owner
At Your Service
459 Lytle Street
Cincinnati, OH 45204

Dear Mr. Welles:

Thank you for agreeing to assist me with my search. Your help is much appreciated!

To give you a bit of background—I graduated from Xavier two years ago and since then have continued to work in the restaurant business. This experience has taught me valuable skills, such as decision-making, customer service, and good communication. But I am ready to put my education (in accounting) to work, and I hope to get your insights into opportunities at your company or elsewhere in this area.

I will call you in a day or two to see when it might be convenient for us to meet.

Again, thanks!

Yours truly,

Amanda Klein

enclosure

Letter 26: No Interview Is Scheduled

Comments: Sharon has been unable to reach Mr. Desmond by phone, but she will persist in trying to make contact. Her letter contains solid and specific examples of her abilities.

Sharon Steiger

2490 Calumet Farm Drive, Cincinnati, OH 45249
513-204-7902 (Mobile)
s_steiger@cinci.rr.com

March 15, 2005

Mr. Brandon Desmond
Chief Information Officer
Cincinnati Financial Services, Inc.
249 Vine Street
Cincinnati, OH 45202

Dear Mr. Desmond:

Following up on my recent phone messages, I am contacting you at the suggestion of Audra Pederson, who has told me about your expansion plans and need for experienced IT leadership.

Leading technology projects, teams, and organizations to support strategic business goals is what I do best. As Senior Technology Leader for Midwest Trust, I guided the massive technology conversion and integration projects that followed each of our 12 acquisitions— in each case, merging hundreds of financial products, systems, and services into our central technology systems, while providing a seamless transition to customers.

Just as importantly, my division supported business growth from $500 million to $6 billion with only a 25% increase in IT staff.

Of course, technology services are only as good as the technical staff that designs, implements, and supports them. I have found that there is no "trick" to keeping staff morale high and turnover low—rather, it relies on a top-down management attitude of respect, empowerment, continuous professional development, and teamwork. The proof of this approach can be seen in the 5% or lower turnover rate I maintained for over a decade.

I'd like to meet and discuss ways in which my leadership, technical, and managerial skills can be valuable to your organization. You may reach me at the above number; I will try to reach you by phone again in the next few days.

Sincerely,

Sharon Steiger

enclosure: resume

Letter 27: No Interview Is Scheduled

Comments: Notice how this letter is a follow-up to a personal meeting at a professional association function. This is an excellent way to make initial contact that you can pursue afterwards with a more focused message. Because Allan is already on a first-name basis with Carol, he uses her first name in the salutation.

Allan P. Raymond, CPA

29 Brookside Drive, Mystic, CT 06433
860.239.7671 • allanraymond@verizon.net

March 15, 2005

Carol P. Graves, CPA
President, Graves & Andrews
254 Court Street
New London, CT 06320

Dear Carol:

I enjoyed our conversation at the recent CPA Society meeting and, as you suggested, I am forwarding my resume with this letter of interest in joining your firm.

You and I agreed that your clients deserve the best: the best accountants, the best strategies, and the greatest dedication to customer service. I am confident I can bring "the best" in both attitude and execution to your firm.

With more than ten years of accounting experience—the last five as a CPA and owner of an accounting firm specializing in tax—I have strong and well-proven professional skills. I thrive on the challenges and intricacies of tax accounting and stay up-to-date with tax code changes through both in-person and online training programs.

What satisfies me most in my professional life is the opportunity to help clients better manage, control, and benefit from their money. One of the keys to the good advice I give my clients is my deep understanding of the consequences of investment decisions on their tax situation. I have worked with businesses of all sizes from one person to complex multimillion-dollar organizations in diverse industries and have contributed strategies and planning recommendations as well as tax-related accounting services.

Having just concluded the sale of my business, I am eager for new professional challenges. I would like to explore my value as a tax accountant with your firm, and in pursuit of that objective I will call you next week to schedule a meeting. Thank you.

Best regards,

Allan P. Raymond

enclosure: resume

Letter 28: No Interview Is Scheduled

Comments: Impressive results are included in the first paragraph to get attention in this blind-ad response.

Rafael Lewis

294 Aster Lane, Cincinnati, OH 45208
Home: (513) 739-1265 • Mobile: (513) 230-0943 • Email: raflewis@hotmail.com

March 30, 2005

Enquirer Box 719-A
Cincinnati, OH 45202

Re: CUSTOMER SERVICE MANAGER

Under my leadership, the customer service department of Tech-Line was transformed from a business liability to a competitive advantage for the company. We cut hold times by 75% and consistently performed at 95% of the world-class standard of 24-hour problem resolution.

As detailed in the enclosed resume, my background includes more than eight years of management experience complemented by a strong technical background in applications development. In all of my positions, I have developed solid collaborative relationships with business and technical departments of the company, and I have consistently demonstrated a customer-centric approach that is also sensitive to bottom-line priorities.

I can be a valuable addition to your team and look forward to a personal meeting to discuss how I can deliver results for your company.

Sincerely,

Rafael Lewis

enclosure

Letter 29: No Interview Is Scheduled

Comments: This promising contact came about as a result of a professional association meeting. The letter focuses on results and relates to the needs of the reader and his organization.

JANINE T. McGUIRE

512-349-1265   749-A Whistler Court, Austin, TX 78714   jtm@austin.rr.com

---

March 15, 2005

Robert Smith
Vice President of Operations
Sanibel Systems, Inc.
4545 Round Rock Parkway
Austin, TX 78710

Dear Mr. Smith:

You will recall that we spoke briefly after your presentation at the Austin Business Leaders Forum last week, when I followed up on your comments about expanding your materials management organization. As you suggested, I am providing additional background material and will call in a few days to set up a meeting.

Throughout my career in materials, logistics, and procurement, I have delivered results such as these:

- 99.3% on-time delivery, $1.5 million in cost savings, and $2.5 million in inventory reduction in 18 months as Director of Purchasing and Materials Management for a technology supplier

- Creation of a world-class purchasing group at Apex Technology—by reengineering functions and aligning activities with strategic business goals

- Key contributions to growth and profitability that spurred the emergence of Intelli-Tech as a world-leading technology supplier

- Consistent cost reductions in tandem with quality and service improvements through innovative value-stream, value-added strategies

My experience in lean global sourcing, value-enhanced supply-chain operations, and management of outsourcing initiatives can help Sanibel as you face tough challenges in today's competitive global economy. One of my strengths is negotiating contracts and managing relationships with contract manufacturers, consultants, and outsource technology providers (I can help you get the most "bang for the buck" in short- and long-term). I am fully conversant in all facets of Lean Materials Management, Purchasing, and Manufacturing; I excel in high-responsibility positions and am Kaizen process oriented.

I appreciate your willingness to meet with me. I will call you shortly to set it up.

Sincerely,

Janine T. McGuire

Enclosure: resume

Letter 30: No Interview Is Scheduled

Comments: The focal point of this letter is the list of impressive results. The letter also provides a good explanation for why the candidate is looking for a job. Notice that Chris called the recruiting firm before sending a cover letter and resume.

Chris Angelos
152 Elm Street, Reading, MA 01867 • (H) 781-942-0925 • (M) 781-204-9904 • angelos@verizon.net

March 15, 2005

Steven T. Edgerton
Executive Search Consultant
Biggs, Byers, Bailey & Bloggs
859 Madison Avenue, Suite 21B
New York, NY 10023

Dear Mr. Edgerton:

Thank you for spending some time on the phone with me today. Your firm's reputation as a leader in manufacturing-industry searches prompted my call, and I was glad to learn that you have several active searches that might fit my profile.

Building productivity, profitability, and efficiency in manufacturing operations is what I do best. For the past six years, I have led a custom-aluminum manufacturer to consistently high profitability while delivering strong results in all areas of operations:

- 100% key customer satisfaction
- 100% on-time delivery for our top account
- 100% environmental regulatory compliance
- 99+% quality
- 83% reduction in production downtime
- 25% reduction in inventory
- 15%, 20%, and 25% reductions in product, service, and utility costs
- 10% sales growth with all major accounts

As a hands-on manager, I have practical working knowledge of every area of operations. I have instilled a "customer first" attitude top to bottom throughout the plant. My work ethic and reliability are exceptional (I haven't missed a scheduled day of work in 15 years), and I enjoy the challenge of continuously improving an already good operation.

The owner's decision to increase his own involvement and bring additional family members into the business is the reason for my current search. My record shows what I have done for the bottom line and our customers; I'm confident I can do the same as a Plant Manager or Production Supervisor for one of your clients.

I would like to schedule a meeting with you on my next trip to New York, and I will call you on Friday to find a convenient time.

Sincerely,

Chris Angelos

enclosure: resume

Letter 31: No Interview Is Scheduled

Comments: Matthew "drops" the name of his referral source in the very first sentence. Notice how specific he is about ways he can help the company.

MATTHEW TAYLOR

2730 Carmel Court		Home 317-249-2187
Indianapolis, IN 46213	mtaylor@earthlink.net	Mobile 317-908-2376

March 15, 2005

Shandra Keeley
Vice President of Operations
Hoosier Building Materials, Inc.
7619 Victory Parkway
Indianapolis, IN 46210

Dear Ms. Keeley:

Stan Asher, store manager of the Carmel Home Depot, suggested I contact you; he thought you would be interested in my background and my ability to help Hoosier Building Materials grow.

In operations management roles with Midwest Windows, I cut inventory levels 40%, set company records for shipping volume, trimmed 15% from our fleet expenses, and more than doubled inventory turns—all in the last two years.

I could deliver similar results for your organization. Specifically, I can help you in four ways:

1. **Operational Improvement...** transforming underperformers to top-of-the-class operations... striving for continuous improvement through ongoing, aggressive initiatives.
2. **Team Building...** taking over entrenched organizations and creating motivated, nimble teams that quickly respond to changing business demands.
3. **Financial Performance...** driving cost from all areas of manufacturing and distribution operations.
4. **Operational Systems and Controls...** creating the essential foundation for business growth.

My experience is diverse and includes hands-on leadership of marketing, sales, product development, manufacturing, finance, forecasting/budgeting, IT, and logistics. The key to success in every role has been my ability to build relationships, both internally and externally, and to create support for new initiatives and new ways of doing business. The results have exceeded expectations and opened new opportunities for growth.

I would like to meet with you to explore how I can deliver bottom-line benefits to Hoosier in an operations leadership role. I will call you next week in hopes of setting up a meeting.

Thank you.

Sincerely,

Matthew Taylor

enclosure: resume

Letter 32: No Interview Is Scheduled

Comments: This letter is written to a network contact who is now in the position of screening candidates for a specific opportunity.

Dear Donald,

It has been a pleasure speaking with you about the Schram Health Center executive director position, and I appreciate your guidance.

As requested, I am attaching my resume. These brief highlights of my qualifications will give you an idea of the value I can bring to the Schram Center.

== Six years in Director-level roles with Southwest Medical Center, delivering results in the most challenging of climates.

== Proven ability to lead key strategic initiatives from concept to successful conclusion. Success stories at Southwest include developing a master plan, launching a new campus, and introducing family-centered care hospital-wide.

== Deep understanding of the intricacies of diverse healthcare entities, including hospitals, satellite facilities, and mental health operations… and deep commitment to making a difference through effective leadership of these organizations.

== Talent for working with boards, community sponsors, and all members of the healthcare team to deliver the best possible services to our various constituents.

== MBA and BSBA degrees.

I will be happy to prepare a more detailed cover letter explaining my qualifications—and, I hope, communicating my passion—as soon as I have the opportunity to review your package of materials; I look forward to receiving that from you as soon as it is ready.

Again, Donald, thank you for your assistance. I am excited about this opportunity and eager to share my ideas with the Schram Center executives and board members.

Sincerely,

Alex Rivera

Letter 33: No Interview Is Scheduled

Comments: This job seeker uses a quote as an attention-getter in "cold-calling" a senior executive.

LINDSEY CARMICHAEL
21 Hillside Drive, Novato, CA 94949
415-245-1265   lindsey@home.net

March 15, 2005

Alden Gaines
Vice President, Operations
Columbia Products, Inc.
9495 Industrial Parkway
Newark, NJ 07184

Dear Mr. Gaines:

Recently, you were quoted as saying, "Cost-effective management of your company's supply chain operations can mean the difference between profit and loss."

I couldn't agree more, and I would like to talk with you about how I can help your company in this regard.

I have a track record of innovative and successful management of large-scale transportation and logistics operations, and I know how to plan, implement, and manage the supply chain for maximum business benefit—both immediate and long range. Consider these highlights:

- In my current position, I have just completed laying the groundwork for a global distribution initiative that projects savings of $5 million annually.

- With Bayou Chemical, I captured $7 million in savings in less than two years through effective management of our logistics resources.

- Previously, charged with setting up the transportation/distribution function at a newly acquired plant, I established the foundation for a very cost-effective logistics program that has contributed to record-high profitability at that plant.

The reason I am contacting you is that family priorities dictate that I relocate to the Northeast, so I am searching for a new professional challenge. Your words inspired me to think that I could find that challenge at Columbia Products—or that you may know of another company in the area that could use my expertise. I will call next week to determine whether you have an interest.

Thank you.

Sincerely,

Lindsey Carmichael

enclosure

Letter 34: Pre-Interview, for a Specific Job Opening

Comments: The last paragraph suggests that Richard is already thinking about ways to help his prospective new company.

RICHARD TALLANT

rtallant@earthlink.net

206-595-2781 Home • 206-218-8712 Mobile
3909 43rd Street NE, Seattle, WA 98128

March 30, 2005

John P. Edmonds
President, Pharmedic Networks, Inc.
2912 Second Street
Seattle, WA 98108

Dear Mr. Edmonds:

Thank you for taking my call today. I was pleased to discover that you might have a need for an executive with my experience and track record, and I look forward to meeting you on Wednesday.

As we discussed, I have been successful building profitable companies in today's dynamic healthcare market—growing revenues, outperforming profit goals, and achieving dominant market position for diverse organizations that include start-ups, multiple mergers, and regional expansions. For example:

- As Senior VP for the Northwest Region of an expanding services organization, I led a performance turnaround that resulted in 225% revenue growth and 353% increase in operating income.

- Previously, as Operations VP, I orchestrated the smooth integration of 10 companies into a cohesive organization—all the while adding new institutional customers and expanding into new service lines.

- In the emerging arena of pharmacy services to the LTC market, I played the lead role in growing a single-site company to a highly profitable regional leader with 45 sites.

I offer strong sales/marketing and operations leadership skills and the proven ability to drive growth and improvement. The result is a tightly run, clearly focused organization whose people "own" the vision and communicate the brand value at every customer interaction. My deep knowledge of the healthcare industry (long term care services, managed care, insurance, healthcare technology) is the foundation for innovative vision, practical strategy, and the ability to spot opportunities.

When we meet, I'd like to share with you some ideas I have for growing both your pharmacy services and your medical supplies operations. Thank you, again, for your interest.

Sincerely,

Richard Tallant

enclosure: resume

Additional Job Search Correspondence: Thank-You Letters, Quick Notes, JIST Cards, Job Proposals, and More

Much of the information in this chapter is often overlooked in resume books and by job seekers. That is too bad, because in our experience thank-you notes are a very effective job search tool. So are JIST Cards, a mini-resume that you will soon learn about. Other related correspondence can also play an important part in a quick, successful job search.

Thank-You Notes

While resumes and cover letters get the attention, thank-you notes often get results. That's right. Sending thank-you notes makes both good manners and good job search sense. When used properly, thank-you notes can help you build on the positive impression you created during your interview or phone discussion. They can help make you more memorable to hiring managers. And they might even sway a hiring manager who is "on the fence" to include you in the next round of interviews.

Three Times When You Should Definitely Send Thank-You Notes—and Why

Thank-you notes have a more intimate and friendly social tradition than formal business correspondence. I think that is one reason they work so well—people respond to those who show good manners and say thank you. Here are some situations when you should use them, along with some sample notes.

1. Before an Interview

In some situations, you can send a less formal note before an interview, usually by e-mail unless the interview is scheduled for a fairly distant future date. For example, you can simply thank someone for being willing to see you. Depending on the situation, enclosing a resume could be a bit inappropriate. Remember, this is supposed to be sincere thanks for help and not an assertive business situation. This also serves as a way to confirm the date and time of the scheduled interview and as a gentle reminder to the recipient that you will be showing up at that time. Figure 4-1 is an example of a thank-you note written for such an occasion.

Figure 4-1: Sample Thank-You Note Sent Before an Interview

April 5, 20XX

Ms. Kijek,

Thanks so much for your willingness to see me next Wednesday at 9 a.m.

I know that I am one of many who are interested in working with your organization, but I'm confident that you'll find my qualifications are a good fit for the role. I've enclosed a JIST Card that presents the basics of my skills for this job and will bring my resume to the interview.

I appreciate the opportunity to meet you and learn more about the position. Please call me if you have any questions at all.

Sincerely,

Bruce Vernon

2. After an Interview

One of the best times to send a thank-you note is right after an interview. Here are several reasons why:

- Doing so creates a positive impression. The employer will assume you have good follow-up skills—to say nothing of good manners.

- It creates yet another opportunity for you to remain in the employer's consciousness at an important time.

- It gives you a chance to get in the last word. You get to include a subtle reminder of why you're the best candidate for the job and can even address any concerns that might have come up during the interview.

- Should they have buried, passed along, or otherwise lost your resume and previous correspondence, a thank-you note and corresponding JIST Card provide one more chance for employers to find your number and call you.

> **Tip:** *Enclose a JIST Card with your thank-you notes when sending your note through the mail—you can find JIST Card samples and writing tips later in this chapter. JIST Cards fit well into a thank-you-note-sized envelope, and they provide key information an employer can use to contact you. JIST Cards also list key skills and other credentials that will help you create a good impression. And the employer could always forward the card to someone who might have a job opening for you.*

For these reasons, we suggest you send a thank-you note right after the interview, and certainly within 24 hours. Figure 4-2 is an example of such a note.

Figure 4-2: Sample Thank-You Note Sent After an Interview

August 11, 20XX

Dear Mr. O'Beel,

Thank you for the opportunity to interview for the position available in your production department. I want you to know that this is the sort of job I have been looking for and I am enthusiastic about the possibility of working for you.

Now that we have spoken, I know that I have both the experience and skills to fit nicely into your organization and to be productive quickly. The process improvements I implemented at Logistics, Inc., increased their productivity 34%, and I'm confident that I could do the same for you.

Thanks again for the interview; I enjoyed the visit.

Sara Smith

(505) 665-0090

3. Whenever Anyone Helps You in Your Job Search

Send a thank-you note to anyone who helps you during your job search. This includes those who give you referrals, people who provide advice, or simply those who are supportive during your search. We suggest you routinely enclose one or more JIST Cards in these notes because recipients can give them to others who may be in a better position to help you. Figure 4-3 is an example of such a note.

> **Tip:** *Send a thank-you note by e-mail or mail as soon as possible after an interview or meeting. This is when you are freshest in the mind of the person who receives it and are most likely to make a good impression.*

Figure 4-3: Sample Thank-You Note to Someone Who Helped in the Job Search

October 31, 20XX
2234 Riverbed Ave.
Philadelphia, PA 17963

Ms. Helen A. Colcord
Henderson and Associates, Inc.
1801 Washington Blvd., Suite 1201
Philadelphia, PA 17963

Dear Ms. Colcord,

Thank you for sharing your time with me so generously yesterday. I really appreciated talking to you about your career field.

The information you shared with me increased my desire to work in such an area. Your advice has already proven helpful—I have an appointment to meet with Robert Hopper on Friday.

In case you think of someone else who might need a person like me, I'm enclosing another resume and JIST Card.

Sincerely,

Debbie Childs

Nine Quick Tips for Writing Thank-You Notes

Here are some brief tips to help you write your thank-you notes.

1. Decide Whether E-mail or Snail Mail Makes More Sense

Consider the timing involved and the formality of the person and organization you're sending it to. If you need to get a letter out quickly because it has to arrive before an interview that's coming up soon, or if it's a thank-you note after an interview and you know the employer will be making a decision soon, then e-mail is your best bet. Use regular mail if there's no rush and if you sense that the other person would appreciate the formality of a business letter printed on nice paper and received in the mail.

2. Use High-Quality Paper and Envelopes

Use good quality notepaper with matching envelopes. Most stationery stores have thank-you note cards and envelopes in a variety of styles. Select a note that is simple and professional—avoid cute graphics and sayings. A blank card or simple "Thank You" on the front will do. For a professional look, match your thank-you note paper to your resume. We suggest off-white and buff colors.

3. Handwritten or Typed Is Acceptable

Traditionally, thank-you notes were handwritten, but most are typed (word-processed) these days. If your handwriting is good and your thank-you note is short, it is perfectly acceptable to write it. In fact, this can be a nice touch. But if your handwriting is hard to read, or if your letter includes more than a couple of brief paragraphs, you will create a better impression by using your word processor. Be sure to match the style and format to your cover letter and resume.

4. Use a Formal Salutation

Don't use a first name unless you are already on a first-name basis with the person you are thanking. Use "Dear Ms. Smith" or "Ms. Smith" rather than the less formal "Dear Pam." Include the date.

5. Keep the Note Informal and Friendly

Keep your note short and friendly. Remember, the note is a thank-you for what someone else did, not a hard-sell pitch for what you want. Make sure, though, that in a thank-you note after an interview you remind your audience of your skills or other qualifications that are relevant to the job. This lets the thank-you note serve as not only an expression of appreciation but also as a chance to get the last word on why you should be hired. The more savvy members of your competition will be doing this, so you had better do it, too.

Also, make sure your thank-you note does not sound like a form letter. Put some time and effort into it to tailor it to the recipient and the situation.

6. Tell How You Will Follow Up

As appropriate, be specific about when you will next contact the person. If you plan to meet soon, still send a note saying you look forward to the meeting and say thank you for the appointment. And make sure that you include something to remind the employer of who you are and how to reach you, since your name alone may not be enough to be remembered.

7. Sign It

Sign your first and last name. Avoid initials and make your signature legible.

8. Send It Right Away

Write and send your note no later than 24 hours after you make your contact. Ideally, you should write it immediately after the contact, while the details are fresh in your mind.

9. Enclose a JIST Card

Depending on the situation, a JIST Card is often the ideal enclosure to include with a thank-you note. It's small, it's soft sell, and it provides your contact information, should the employer wish to reach you. It is both a reminder of you, should any jobs open up, and a tool to pass along to someone else. Make sure your thank-you notes and envelopes are big enough to enclose an unfolded JIST Card.

More Sample Thank-You Notes

Following are a few more samples of thank-you notes and letters. They cover a variety of situations and will give you ideas on how to structure your own correspondence. Notice that they are all short and friendly, and typically mention that the writer will follow up in the future—a key element of a successful job search campaign.

Also note that several are following up on interviews where no specific job opening exists—yet. As we've mentioned elsewhere in this book, getting interviews before a job opening exists is a very smart thing to do.

Figure 4-4: After an Informational Interview

Comments: This letter is a follow-up to an informational meeting with a person who has already provided some referrals and might be in a position to provide even more.

RICHARD TALLANT

rtallant@earthlink.net

206-595-2781 Home • 206-218-8712 Mobile
3909 43rd Street NE, Seattle, WA 98128

March 30, 2005

John P. Edmonds
President, Pharmedic Networks, Inc.
2912 Second Street
Seattle, WA 98108

Dear Mr. Edmonds:

Thank you for taking my call today. I was pleased to discover that you might have a need for an executive with my experience and track record, and I look forward to meeting you on Wednesday.

As we discussed, I have been successful building profitable companies in today's dynamic healthcare market growing revenues, outperforming profit goals, and achieving dominant market position in diverse organizations that include start-ups, multiple mergers, and regional expansions. For example:

- As Senior VP for the Northwest Region of an expanding services organization, I led a performance turnaround that resulted in 225% revenue growth and 353% increase in operating income.

- Previously, as Operations VP, I orchestrated the smooth integration of 10 companies into a cohesive organization—all the while adding new institutional customers and expanding into new service lines.

- In the emerging arena of pharmacy services to the LTC market, I played the lead role in growing a single-site company to a highly profitable regional leader with 45 sites.

I offer strong sales/marketing and operations leadership skills and the proven ability to drive growth and improvement. The result is a tightly run, clearly focused organization whose people "own" the vision and communicate the brand value at every customer interaction. My deep knowledge of the healthcare industry (long term care services, managed care, insurance, healthcare technology) is the foundation for innovative vision, practical strategy, and the ability to spot opportunities.

When we meet, I'd like to share with you some ideas I have for growing both your pharmacy services and your medical supplies operations. Thank you, again, for your interest.

Sincerely,

Richard Tallant

enclosure: resume

Figure 4-5: To Someone Who Has Been Helpful

Comments: Notice how Allan has been able to return the favor to this person who was helpful in his job search.

Allan P. Raymond, CPA
29 Brookside Drive, Mystic, CT 06433
860.239.7671 • allanraymond@verizon.net

March 30, 2005

Ellen Farmer
President, Sound Financial
112 Front Street
New London, CT 06321

Dear Ms. Farmer:

Thank you for taking the time to meet with me. Your ideas were excellent, and I have already reached out to both of the contacts you suggested. Like you, both Mr. Avenida and Mr. Stroman felt that my background makes me a great fit for a small- to medium-sized CPA firm that needs an experienced professional. I am vigorously pursuing all leads and hope that you will keep me in mind as you interact with various business leaders in the New London area.

To that end, I have enclosed a few JIST Cards that are a convenient way for you to pass along my credentials.

As a small way of returning the favor, I have given your name and business cards to two people I know who are in financial transition (Mary McCormick is getting a divorce, and Chris Taylor recently came into a small inheritance) and suggested they give you a call. From what you told me, your services would be a great fit for their special circumstances.

If I can be of further help to you, please let me know. And as you suggested, I will follow up with you from time to time to keep you informed of my progress. Thanks so much!

Best regards,

Allan P. Raymond

enclosures

Figure 4-6: No Opening Currently Exists

Comments: In this letter, Janine makes the case for hiring her even though an opening does not currently exist. Her "pitch" is soft-sell, professional, and focused on the employer's and client's needs.

JANINE T. MCGUIRE

512-349-1265   749-A Whistler Court, Austin, TX 78714   jtm@austin.rr.com

---

March 30, 2005

Robert Smith
Vice President of Operations
Sanibel Systems, Inc.
4545 Round Rock Parkway
Austin, TX 78710

Dear Bob:

The information you shared at our meeting today was extremely helpful, and I am very grateful.

I appreciate that you will keep me in mind for a project leadership role with your company. I am quite willing to start on an interim, as-needed basis; I am sure I will be able to prove very quickly that I offer great value to your firm and your clients.

In particular, Bob, your upcoming work for Bedrock Systems is very close to my experience with Apex. As you will recall, I led a reengineering project with the purchasing department to bring activities and initiatives in line with the company's strategic goals. The results were remarkable ($4 million in cost savings in 18 months) and are directly related to Bedrock's current needs and challenges.

I will keep in touch, Bob, and hope you will call on me if there is some way I can be of help.

Most sincerely,

Janine T. McGuire

Figure 4-7: To Build a Relationship

Comments: With this letter, Jamie is building a relationship that can be of help—if not immediately, then in the future. Note the P.S., which shows creative thinking while providing some helpful information to the company.

Jamie Van Horn

253 Silverton Trail, Phoenix, AZ 85017
602-779-1682 • jvanhorn@yahoo.com

March 30, 2005

Sally Osborne
Southwest District Manager
Pfizer Pharmaceuticals
6512 Scottsdale Boulevard
Phoenix, AZ 85010

Dear Ms. Osborne:

You have confirmed my belief that a pharmaceutical sales career is a great fit for my talents and interests! I really appreciate the time and information you shared with me today.

I understand that there are no current openings in your Southwest District. Of course, I would be pleased to remain here in Phoenix, but I am very open to relocating, and I understand that it is often necessary to move around a bit as one gets established in this field.

Thank you for offering to share my information with others at your company. To make this easy for you, I am enclosing several JIST Cards and extra copies of my resume.

Again, thank you. I will keep in touch.

Very truly yours,

Jamie Van Horn

enclosures

P.S.   Thinking about the marketing challenges we discussed for your new drug Top-ex, it seems to me that a good way to gain exposure while doing good would be to provide samples for homeless shelters. Foot problems related to diabetes are a real issue for the homeless population. Perhaps you have thought of this already—but if not, I think it is worth studying!

Figure 4-8: Reinforcing "Fit"

Comments: This brief note reinforces the candidate's "fit" with the culture of the company he is targeting. It is always a good strategy to keep in touch with your contacts and to get their permission to do so during your meeting, even if they do not think they will be able to hire you.

March 30, 2005

Dear Samantha,

I know how busy you are, and I am extremely grateful that you were willing to share some time with me on Monday.

I realize that you do not have an opening for me at this time, but I am very interested in joining the Armanda team. From my research, backed up by what you told me on Monday, it is a great fit for not only my skills and expertise, but my preferred work style as well. There is nothing that motivates me more than a tough challenge and a tight deadline!

As you suggested, I will touch base with you in about a month to see whether things have changed.

In the meantime, if there is any way that I can be of help to you, please let me know.

Sincerely,

Ryder Wilson

Figure 4-9: Asking for the Job

Comments: In keeping with the need for salespeople to be assertive, this letter is a rather bold request for the job.

Kathy Miller

2943 Hillside Street, Unit 2-B ▪ Oakland, California 94624 ▪ 510-245-7450 ▪ kathymiller@verizon.net

March 30, 2005

Steve Rostakoff
Western Regional Manager
NuTraders Network
9090 Mile High Drive
Denver, CO 80209

Dear Steve:

NuTraders has an exciting future, and I would like to help the Institutional Services division skyrocket to a market-dominant position in the West.

NuTraders' new offerings put the company in a short-term position of market advantage. To seize this advantage requires a "hit the ground running" sales approach. As we discussed, my experience with Schwab closely parallels your new Western Sales Manager position. I know the market... I know the key players... I know the industry and the products... and I have the experience and track record to deliver both immediate revenue results and sustainable long-term growth.

With the right person at the helm, the first-year goal of $100 million in sales is easily reachable. I believe I am that person. I hope you agree.

As you requested, I am attaching a list of professional references, and I will follow up with you on April 6 to see whether you have any additional questions. Thank you for sharing so much time and information with me this week; I am inspired by your enthusiasm and eager to play a part in building a strong Western Region for NuTraders.

Sincerely,

Kathy Miller

enclosure

Quick Notes vs. Formal Cover Letters

Most of this book addresses how to write the formal cover letters that will accompany your resume on most occasions. Earlier we mentioned that a quick note can take the place of a cover letter and be just as effective.

A quick note (or e-mail message) can be sent, along with your resume, to a friend or network contact after a conversation. A quick note can accompany a newspaper article or other item that you send to someone you know or someone you've met with. Quick notes are informal and short. Here are a few examples:

> *Jerry, thanks for suggesting I speak with Reggie Tyler. We are meeting next Friday and I will keep you in the loop! In the meantime, I am attaching my resume in case you have the occasion to pass it on. I appreciate all of your help.*

> *Laura, congratulations on the great press coverage! You might like this extra copy for your files. I am eager to share my job search progress with you—I will give you a call soon.*

> *Bob—Thought you'd enjoy this article. It is right in line with our recent conversation. Would you have a few minutes to talk later this week? I will call to set it up.*

> *Terri, it was good to see you today. As you suggested, here is my resume. I'll call to see whether you might be able to get away for a cup of coffee on Friday. I'd love to get your ideas and insights.*

Here are some thoughts to keep in mind as you write and use quick notes:

- **A quick, informal note should never be sent to someone you don't know.** In those instances, a formal cover letter is more appropriate.

Note: *You should consider sending quick notes or letters to anyone who helps you in your job search. This includes those who simply give you the name of someone to contact or who spoke with you on the phone. Besides showing good manners, it provides you with an opportunity to provide additional information about yourself via an enclosed resume and JIST Card (which people can pass along to others). It will also help to keep your needs in others' minds.*

- **Quick notes must be short.** If you are writing more than three or four sentences, use a letter instead.

- **Quick notes are a great way to stay in contact with people in your network.** They are no-response-required communications that put no pressure on your contacts.

JIST Cards—A Mini-Resume and a Powerful Job Search Tool

JIST Cards are a job search tool that gets results. I (Mike Farr, one of this book's authors) first developed them many years ago, almost by accident. I helped job seekers create them to get attention and "leave something behind" after dropping in without appointments to ask for interviews with employers. Many thousands of job seekers have used them in every imaginable print and electronic format and they still get attention—and interviews—that more traditional tools do not.

A JIST Card is carefully constructed to contain all the essential information most employers want to know in a very short format. It typically uses a 3 × 5–inch card format, but has been designed into many other sizes and formats, such as a folded business card.

Your JIST Card can be as simple as handwritten or created with graphics and on special papers. You create a JIST Card in addition to a resume because a JIST Card is used in a different way.

JIST Cards Get Results

What matters is what JIST Cards accomplish—they get results. In our surveys of employers, more than 90 percent of people receiving JIST Cards form a positive impression of the writer within 30 seconds. More amazing is that about 80 percent of employers say they would be willing to interview the person behind the JIST Card, even if they did not have a job opening now.

How You Can Use Them

You can use a JIST Card in many ways, including the following:

- Attached to your resume or application
- Enclosed in a thank-you note

- Given to your friends, relatives, and other contacts—so they can give them to other people

- Sent out to everyone who graduated from your school or who are members of a professional association

- Put on car windshields

- Posted on the supermarket bulletin board

- In electronic form as an e-mail or e-mail attachment

We are not kidding about finding JIST Cards on windshields or bulletin boards. They can be included on Web sites along with your resume or included as text or attachments in e-mail to people you know, with a request to forward it to others. We've seen them used in these ways and hear about more ways people are using them all the time.

Writing Your JIST Card

A JIST Card is small, so it can't contain many details. It should list only the information that is most important to employers. To write your card, follow these steps:

> **Tip:** JIST Cards are an effective job search tool! Give them to friends and network contacts. Attach one to a resume. Enclose them in your thank-you notes before or after an interview. Leave one with an employer as a business card. Send one as an e-mail or e-mail attach-ment for people to forward to others. Use them in many creative ways. Put lots of them into circulation.

1. **Type your name at the top of the card.** You can center it and use bold text to make it stand out, as you would on a resume.

2. **Give two ways for the employer to contact you.** Space down a few lines and left-align this information. Generally, all you will need to include is your daytime phone number or cell phone number and your e-mail address.

3. **Give a broad job objective.** Space down another line or two and left-align this information. A broad objective will allow you to be considered for many jobs.

4. **List your years of experience.** Space down again and add one sentence that summarizes how long you have been working in this field.

5. **Detail your education and training.** In the same paragraph, add a sentence that tells what degrees, certifications, diplomas, and other relevant training you have.

6. **Showcase your job-related skills.** Still in the same paragraph, add up to four sentences that tell what you can do and how well you can do it. Be sure to include accomplishments and numbers to support them.

7. **State your availability and preferred working arrangements.** If applicable, space down and add a sentence that states any special availability you might have, such as "interested in part-time work," or "available with two weeks' notice."

> **Note:** *JIST Cards are harder to write than they look. The foundation for a JIST Card is an effective resume. Be sure to check out chapter 5 for quick ways to improve your resume, then create your JIST Cards and use them by the score. They work, but only if they are in circulation.*

8. **End with your key adaptive skills.** Space down a few more lines and add one last sentence that tells what personality traits you have that make you a good employee.

JIST Card Paper and Format Tips

Many office-supply stores have perforated light card-stock sheets to run through your computer printer. These will then tear apart into 3 × 5–inch cards. Many word-processing programs have templates that allow you to format a 3 × 5–inch card size. You can also use regular-size light card stock—available at office-supply stores—print several cards on a sheet, and cut it to the size you need. Print shops can also photocopy or print them in the size you need. Get a few hundred at a time. They are cheap, and the point is to get lots of them in circulation.

Sample JIST Cards

The following sample JIST Cards use a plain format, but you can make them as fancy as you want. So be creative. Look over the examples to see how they are constructed. Some are for entry-level jobs and some are for more advanced ones.

Sandy Nolan

Position: General Office/Clerical

Message: (512) 232-9213

More than two years of work experience plus one year of training in office practices. Type 55 wpm, trained in word processing, post general ledger, have good interpersonal skills, and get along with most people. Can meet deadlines and handle pressure well.

Willing to work any hours.

Organized, honest, reliable, and hardworking.

Joyce Hua   **Home: (214) 173-1659**
                                                       Message: (214) 274-1436
                                                       Email: jhua@yahoo.com

Position: Programming/Systems Analyst

More than 10 years of combined education and experience in data processing and related fields. Competent programming in Visual Basic, C, C++, FORTRAN, and Java, and database management. Extensive PC network applications experience. Have supervised a staff as large as seven on special projects and have a record of meeting deadlines. Operations background in management, sales, and accounting.

Desire career-oriented position, will relocate.

Dedicated, self-starter, creative problem solver.

Paul Thomas

Home: (301) 681-3922
Message: (301) 681-6966
Cell phone: (301) 927-9856

Position: Research Chemist, Research Management
in a small-to-medium-sized company

Ph.D. in biochemistry plus more than 15 years of work experience. Developed and patented various processes with current commercial applications worth many millions of dollars. Experienced with all phases of lab work with an emphasis on chromatography, isolation, and purification of organic and biochemical compounds. Specialize in practical pharmaceutical and agricultural applications of chemical research. Have teaching, supervision, and project management experience.

Married more than 15 years, stable work history, results and task oriented, ambitious, and willing to relocate.

Richard Straightarrow

Home: (602) 253-9678
Message: (602) 257-6643
E-mail: RSS@email.cmm

Objective: Electronics installation, maintenance, and sales

Four years of work experience plus a two-year A.S. degree in Electronics Engineering Technology. Managed a $360,000/year business while going to school full time, with grades in the top 25%. Familiar with all major electronic diagnostic and repair equipment. Hands-on experience with medical, consumer, communication, and industrial electronics equipment and applications. Good problem-solving and communication skills. Customer service oriented.

Willing to do what it takes to get the job done.

Self motivated, dependable, learn quickly.

Juanita Rodriguez   Message: (639) 361-1754
Email: jrodriguez@email.cmm

Position: Warehouse Management

Six years of experience plus two years of formal business course work. Have supervised a staff as large as 16 people and warehousing operations covering over two acres and valued at more than $14,000,000. Automated inventory operations resulting in a 30% increase in turnover and estimated annual savings more than $250,000. Working knowledge of accounting, computer systems, time and motion studies, and advanced inventory management systems.

Will work any hours.

Responsible, hardworking, and can solve problems.

Deborah Levy   **Home: (213) 432-8064**
Pager: (212) 876-9487

Position: Hotel Management Professional

Four years of experience in sales, catering, and accounting in a 300-room hotel. Associate degree in Hotel Management plus one year with the Boileau Culinary Institute. Doubled revenues from meetings and conferences. Increased dining room and bar revenues by 44%. Have been commended for improving staff productivity and courtesy. I approach my work with industry, imagination, and creative problem-solving skills.

Enthusiastic, well-organized, and detail-oriented.

Jonathan Michael   Cell phone: (614) 788-2434
                                    E-mail: jonn@pike.org

Objective: Management

More than 7 years of management experience plus a B.S. degree in business. Managed budgets as large as $10 million. Experienced in cost control and reduction, cutting more than 20% of overhead while business increased more than 30%. Good organizer and problem solver. Excellent communication skills.

Prefer responsible position in a medium-to-large business.

Cope well with deadline pressure, seek challenge, flexible.

Other Job Search Correspondence

Besides thank-you notes and JIST Cards, you can send a variety of other items to people during your job search. Following are brief comments about some of these ways of communicating with potential employers.

Follow-Up Letters After an Interview

You might wish to send follow-up correspondence after an interview to solve an employer's problem, present a proposal or an idea, or reinforce the case for hiring you. Earlier in this chapter you saw some examples of letters and notes that were sent following an interview, whether or not it was for an available opening. Remember, you want to stay in contact with people who might be able to hire you in the future even if they cannot now. A good way to keep the connection going is to present a proposal or idea that will be of interest to the person you met. Then you can follow up again to discuss your idea of how to solve a problem for them. The sample letter from Jamie Van Horn (page 92) shows one way to suggest an idea.

When you have interviewed for a specific job, your follow-up letter is a prime opportunity to reinforce that you are the right person for that job.

What have you done in the past that makes it likely you will succeed in the new position? These are the items you should emphasize in your follow-up letter. Also share ideas for helping to meet the specific challenges that you discussed during the interview. The sample letter from Kathy Miller (page 94) demonstrates effective follow-up to an interview.

Job Proposals

In some cases, you could submit a much more comprehensive proposal that would essentially justify your job. If a job opening were available, you could submit an outline of what you would do if hired. If no job is available, you could submit a proposal that would create a job and state what you would do to make it pay off.

In writing such a proposal, it is essential that you be specific in telling an employer what you would do and what results these actions would bring. For example, if you propose to increase sales, how would you do it and how much might sales increase? Tell the employer what you could accomplish, and he or she might just create a new position for you. It happens this way more often than you probably realize.

Here are two simple job proposals that clearly show that there is more *benefit* than *cost* to hiring each employee.

Figure 4-10: A Job Proposal for an Installation Assistant

Job Proposal
Installation Assistant for Acme Shutters

Save $100 per day, serve customers faster,
and improve the efficiency of your installation team.

Summary of Situation

Currently your delivery and installation team consists of two people, senior installation specialists who can professionally install both interior and exterior shutters. They earn approximately $30 per hour and average two complete installations per day.

While most of the work on each shutter installation can be done by one person, there are several steps where two people are required for measuring, lifting, and visually checking the installation for evenness and aesthetics.

Proposal

I propose that Acme add a third person to the team: an Installation Assistant. In this role, I would fetch and carry hardware and supplies to the installers. I could drive back to the shop to eliminate down time when equipment breaks or is missing from their supply. I would make each of them more efficient because they would not be pulled off their own job to measure, lift, or check the work of their installation partner.

I am an experienced construction assistant, used to ferrying tools and supplies. In my last job I helped experienced finish carpenters and was recognized for "making our work more efficient." I am a licensed driver and have an excellent work record for attendance and punctuality.

Benefits

Adding an assistant would cost $80 per day, assuming an hourly rate of $10 and an 8-hour day. Based on my observation of the installation team, my services would save them 2 hours per average installation, for savings of $60 per installation (two hours at $30/hour) or $120 per day. Not only that, but their increased efficiency would allow them to start and possibly complete three installations per day rather than two, for added savings and greater customer satisfaction.

I would be pleased to discuss this proposal in more detail at your convenience.

Lawrence Rusk
312-459-1276

Figure 4-11: A Job Proposal for an Outside Sales Representative

Employment Proposal:
    Outside Sales Representative, Ferris Printing

Proposed by:
    Thomas Matthews
    75 Swan Terrace, Pittsfield, MA 01201
    413-754-6612
    tom_matthews@aol.com

BENEFITS TO FERRIS PRINTING:

- Bring in at least $100,000 per year in new business.
- Improve service to your best customers through on-site printing consultation.
- Become primary point of contact for customers, freeing up time of specialized production workers now spent on the phone with customers (at least one hour per day per worker).
- Smooth out business ups and-downs that currently occur because company owner is unable to devote full time to sales.

MY BACKGROUND:

I am an experienced print-shop worker (7 years) who knows how to present print material to the customer. Most recently I have gained sales experience and have been successful in the extremely challenging environment of office-supply sales.

I understand that your customers value quality and efficiency as well as the right price, and I know how to ensure that projects are profitable for you.

I will call you on Friday to discuss this proposal in more detail.

Thank you.

Thomas Matthews

Enclosures

In some cases, along with your correspondence you might want to include items such as a writing or graphic design sample. This can be appropriate, although we advise against sending too much material unless the employer requests it. Never send originals unless you are willing to lose them. Assume, in all cases, that what you send will be kept.

Self-Sticking Notes

You have surely used those little notes that stick to papers, walls, and other things. There's a size usually called "flags" that are smaller and narrower than most of the square stick-on notes you probably use. Some even have an arrow design on them. These can be useful when calling attention to specific points on attachments or to provide additional details.

> **Tip:** Use one or two self-sticking notes at the most. Avoid making your correspondence look like a patchwork quilt.

List of References

Once employers begin to get serious, they may want to contact your references as part of their final screening process. To make this easier for them, we suggest that you prepare a list of people to contact. This list should include the complete name, title, organization, address, e-mail and phone number for each reference. You should include information about how each person knows you. For example, indicate that Ms. Rivera was your immediate supervisor for two years.

If you have any question whether a person will provide you with a positive reference, discuss this in advance so that you know what the individual is likely to say about you. If it is not positive, drop this person from your list.

Lining Up References

Some job seekers are concerned about providing references because their prior employers have strict policies not to disclose anything except dates of employment. No matter what the policy at your prior employers is, it is your responsibility to find four, five, or six people who can provide a detailed reference about your work abilities.

Your references do not have to be prior supervisors or employers. They can be colleagues, subordinates, vendors, customers, prior employees, people who have worked with you on a volunteer effort, or anyone else who has genuine insight into your work abilities. Be sure to ask permission before providing their names and contact information!

We recommend that you take the time to prepare your references by sending them information on the types of jobs you now seek, a current resume, JIST Card, and other details. Give them a reminder call when you anticipate that there is going to be a reference check.

Letters of Reference

To supplement your list of telephone and e-mail references, we suggest you request previous employers and other references to write a letter that you can submit to others when asked. Again, we do not recommend that you provide references or other supplemental information unless you have been asked.

If the letters of reference are positive, the advantages are clear. If a letter is negative or so-so, at least you now know that there is a problem with this reference. Depending on the situation, you might contact this previous employer and negotiate what he or she will say if and when called during a pre-employment check.

Unsolicited Letters Requesting an Interview or Other Assistance

We want to discourage you from sending out unsolicited letters as a primary technique. Even though many job search books recommend sending out lots of unsolicited resumes and cover letters, the evidence is overwhelming that this method does not work for most people. Doing the same thing on the Internet often results in the same outcome. The rare exception is if your skills are very much in demand.

We do think that sending a letter or e-mail to people with whom you share a common bond, such as alumni or members of a professional group, can be reasonably effective. This is particularly so if you are looking for a job in another city or region and you send a letter asking someone to help you by providing names of contacts there. Several of the sample cover letters provide examples of this very technique, and it does work, particularly if you follow up by phone and e-mail.

Here is an example of a "broadcast" letter that was sent to members of an alumni group.

Figure 4-12: An Example Broadcast Letter

SHAWNA TAYLOR

shawna@att.net   4540 Riverview Terrace, Covington, KY 41016
                                                  Home 859-245-0290 – Mobile 859-304-2094

March 30, 2005

Larry Anderson
VP Sales & Marketing
Sensational Software
259-A Research Boulevard
Raleigh, NC 27603

Dear Larry:

May I ask your advice and assistance? I was given your name by the Fuqua alumni office and am hoping to tap into your local network as I seek to return to the Raleigh area.

Since graduating from Fuqua, and completing a 16-month MBA Enterprise Corps assignment in Ghana, I've spent an enjoyable five years in software marketing—developing strategy, evaluating marketing channels, and building strategic alliances.

Now I'm looking for a new challenge, where my proven strengths in strategic market planning can add value to a dynamic organization.

If you know of:

> **An opportunity...** in strategic marketing for a technology company...
> **A company...** that has aggressive growth plans and needs marketing leadership...
> **An individual...** at a technology or other high-growth company who would be interested in my background...

I'd greatly appreciate hearing your ideas and referrals.

My resume (enclosed) gives a comprehensive synopsis of my experience and accomplishments. I welcome your advice and value your expertise as I look for the next exciting career opportunity.

Many thanks... I'll phone in a few days to hear your thoughts.

Best regards,

Shawna Taylor

enclosure

Key Points: Chapter 4

Here's a summary of the key points of this chapter:

- Send thank-you notes to everyone you meet with and everyone who has helped you during your job search.

- Send your thank-you notes immediately—within 24 hours of your meeting.

- For a post-interview note, take the opportunity to build on points made during your meeting. Remind your reader why you are a great fit for the job or the organization.

- Use quick notes as informal communications with people you know or people you've met.

- Create and use JIST Cards—small but powerful communicators that have been proven to get results.

- Compile your reference list carefully and let your references help you with your job search

- Use additional materials such as enclosures, self-sticking notes, job proposals, and broadcast letters and e mails as appropriate—when used with discretion, these can be effective.

- Keep in touch with people who have helped you during your job search to stay at the top of their minds and receive ongoing assistance.

Chapter 5

Improve Your Resume in 15 Minutes

We assumed that you have already developed your resume before choosing this book to help you with cover letters. For that reason, we're not going to tell you step-by-step how to write a resume. We do, however, want to give you some ways to quickly improve your resume and really boost its power and effectiveness.

From looking at literally thousands of resumes every year, we have identified some of the most common problems that cause a resume to be ineffective. And we have concentrated our advice in this chapter on how you can address these specific problems if they exist within your resume.

Sources of Additional Information

You can get more help from published sources of resume information, as well as professional writers and career counselors.

Resume Books

If you want more help than the resume overview this chapter provides, we suggest you consider one or more of the following books by the authors:

- *Same-Day Resume:* Similar in format and approach to *15-Minute Cover Letter* and another part of the *Help in a Hurry* series, this book is brief, with helpful resume advice and good examples (Michael Farr, JIST Publishing).

- *The Quick Resume & Cover Letter Book:* More thorough advice, with a "same-day" resume section followed by tips on writing more sophisticated resumes. Many excellent sample resumes by professional resume writers (Michael Farr, JIST Publishing).

- ***Expert Resumes* series:** A series of books with solid advice and lots of sample resumes related to specific fields and situations, including health care, managers and executives, teachers and educators, career changers, computer and Web jobs, people returning to work, and others (Wendy S. Enelow and Louise M. Kursmark, JIST Publishing).

- Other helpful JIST-published resume books include *America's Top Resumes for America's Top Jobs, Résumé Magic, Gallery of Best Resumes* (series), and others.

All of these and many other JIST resume books are available at www.jist.com or at any bookstore or online retailer.

Professional Resume Writers and Career Counselors

If you want professional help with writing your resume, we suggest that you consult with an expert who belongs to one of the nationally recognized professional resume writer associations noted here. There is a member directory on each Web site that will help you find the help you need.

- Career Masters Institute (www.cminstitute.com)

- National Resume Writers' Association (www.nrwa.com)

- Professional Association of Resume Writers and Career Coaches (www.parw.com)

- Professional Resume Writing and Research Association (www.prwra.com)

Three Ways to Improve Your Resume

The issues we see most often in ineffective resumes relate to clarity, focus, relevance, and appearance. Our advice to counteract these problems is quite simple:

1. Be sure your objective is clear.

2. Highlight your achievements.

3. Format for readability, impact, and clarity.

In the following sections, we explore these areas of advice in more detail and provide samples that illustrate each point. And so that you can improve your resume in about 15 minutes, we've created an exercise for each point.

Be Sure Your Objective Is Clear

Your contacts and employer prospects are often extremely busy. They will appreciate it if you give them a resume they can quickly skim to gather essential information. Right from the top, be sure that it is easy for your readers to understand who you are, what you are good at, and what you want to do.

One way to accomplish this is by leading off your resume with an Objective statement. If you choose this format, *be specific!* A vaguely worded resume is of no help to readers, and it doesn't add any value to your document. Your Objective statement should be crisp and clear. It should include some indication of the benefit you offer, not just the job you want.

Job seekers who "don't want to eliminate anything" or want to "leave themselves open" to whatever comes along usually find that employers are not very responsive. Busy hiring authorities just don't have the time or the interest to figure out what kind of work you can do—that's what you need to know and need to tell them in your job search documents, phone calls, e-mails, and meetings.

A Before-and-After Example

Here is an example Objective statement:

Before:

OBJECTIVE: *A challenging, rewarding position where I can use my education, skills, and experience and where there is opportunity for advancement.*

What's wrong with it: It is vague—what kind of job do you want? It does not state clearly what you have to offer (everyone has some kind of "education, skills, and experience"). It does not communicate value to the employer; instead, it talks about what *you* want ("opportunity for advancement").

> **Tip:** *If you are not sure what kind of job you want, consider exploring your possibilities at greater length before putting together your resume and starting your job search. At the very least, identify the specific skills you want to use so that readers understand at least generally the type of work you want to do. In chapter 6, along with an action plan for a quick job search, you will find a worksheet to help you define your skills. This is an important step before you look for your next job.*

After:

OBJECTIVE: *A position as claims adjuster where my deep knowledge of claims processing will result in faster turnaround, smaller payouts, and greater agent and client satisfaction.*

What's right with it: It is clear and concise, communicates specific expertise, and includes information of value to the employer.

Consider an Alternative to an Objective Statement

Today's resumes usually start off with a Summary of Qualifications or other type of introduction rather than an Objective statement. There are several benefits to using this strategy:

- You can more fully express the value that you have to offer.

- A summary can be longer and more detailed than an Objective.

- You can carefully present just the right information that will position you for the type of jobs you are seeking—in a sense, setting up your reader to expect the information that will follow in the rest of the resume.

- You will appear to be more up-to-date with current trends.

> **Tip:** *A "headline" format (like the one used in the General Manager example) is a great way to quickly communicate who you are. You can use a job title ("General Manager") or a broader functional heading ("Operations/Sales/ Marketing/Logistics"). Use subheadings to call out more specifics that will clue the reader in to your areas of expertise. Most of the resume samples later in this chapter use the headline format. It's attractive and very effective.*

If you choose to use a Summary, once again be certain that your expertise is crystal-clear and related to the job you seek now. Upon reading your summary, your audience should be in no doubt about who you are, what you're good at, and how you can help them. Consider the difference between these two Summaries for the same person:

Before:
Qualifications Summary

- *Superior record of growing sales and increasing profitability*

- *Functional experience in sales, marketing, and logistics*

- *Industry experience in automotive, hospitality, health care, and logistics*

What's wrong with it: We don't know what type of position this person wants, nor at what level.

After:

General Manager

Operations • Sales • Marketing • Logistics

Track record of exceeding goals and building top-performing operations in every assignment during progressive career with national, international, and Fortune 500 companies in automotive, hospitality, health-care, and logistics industries. Strategically focused on profit enhancement through performance improvement. Repeatedly successful meeting diverse challenges including turnaround, integration, ownership change, and structural overhaul.

What's right with it: We now know that this individual is a General Manager. Areas of functional responsibility are spelled out below the title to help the reader. The brief paragraph is loaded with value and benefits for the employer.

15-MINUTE EXERCISE

Review your objective or introduction. Ask yourself the following questions:

- Is my objective clear, precise, and specific? (Does it jump off the page?)

- Can readers immediately tell "who I am" and what I'm good at?

- Have I shown ways that I can benefit an organization?

If not, fill in the blanks of the following formula to create a quick introduction that will be more powerful and clear than your current version.

_____ (Position title) with _____ (years) of experience in
_____ _____ (function or industry). Track record of
____ _____ (key accomplishment areas) and proven
ability to _____ (more accomplishment areas).
_____ (intangible skills area) that _____
(value offered).

Example 1:

Mechanical engineer with 12 years of experience in the automotive industry. Track record of successful, cost-effective product development and proven ability to rapidly adapt designs to meet evolving customer needs. Strong management, communications, and team-building skills that ensure on-time, on-budget project completion.

Example 2:

Radiologic technician with 5 years of experience in both hospital-based and standalone facilities. Proven ability to manage a high patient volume while delivering excellent customer service. Strong technical skills, patient skills, and teamwork abilities that contribute to successful operation of a first-class radiology department.

(continued)

(continued)

> ### *Example 3:*
>
> *Retail manager with 15 years of experience with major retailers (Macy's, Gap, Kmart) and a track record of increasing profitability, reducing staff turnover, improving community relations, and designing creative marketing and merchandising programs. Strong leadership skills and proven ability to create a team culture.*
>
> ### *Example 4:*
>
> *Purchasing professional with 9 years of experience in manufacturing industries. Track record of reducing costs at least 10% per year and proven ability to implement Six Sigma methodologies within the procurement organization. Strong supplier relationship and negotiation skills that result in both immediate benefits and favorable long-term agreements.*

This "fill-in-the-blanks" exercise shows one way to write and present your summary. The sample resumes later in this chapter demonstrate several different approaches. If this exercise doesn't give you the results you want, review the other examples to see whether another style better fits your circumstances. There are no hard-and-fast rules about how to present this information; what's important is that your message is clear, concise, and sharply focused.

Highlight Your Achievements

Consider this: When you write a job description in your resume, you are writing about the duties, tasks, and responsibilities that are assigned to anyone holding that particular job. In fact, anyone holding that job could have the identical paragraph on their resume! How different it is when you write about the *achievements* that are unique to you. Not only do you customize your resume, but you also communicate to a future employer that you performed your job effectively—not just what you were "responsible for," but what you actually did.

A resume that includes only job descriptions is bland and uninformative. A resume that highlights your achievements sizzles! It will put you head and shoulders above the average job seeker.

When describing your accomplishments, once again *be specific*. Include numbers, percentages, and other hard evidence of results. Without these quantified results, your achievements will lack power.

Achievement Statement Examples

Consider the difference between these before-and-after examples.

> **Tip:** *We recommend that you just briefly describe your actual job scope/job duties. It is important to put readers in the picture so that they understand the context of your achievements. But it's not necessary to spell out all the details of your day-to-day job activities. Hiring authorities understand the general responsibilities of most jobs; what they want to know is how you performed in that job. It is far more effective to expand on your achievements and minimize the description of your job duties, rather than the other way around.*

Before:

- *Closed multimillion-dollar deals with top-tier companies.*

After:

- *Closed 60+ deals with top-tier companies (e.g., DaimlerChrysler, Hallmark, Disney) and generated more than $100 million in revenue in first year of product launch.*

Before:

- *Improved accounting processes to increase efficiency and speed up the monthly closing process.*

After:

- *Cut 9 days from monthly close (15 days to 6) and saved $50K in annual labor costs (one full-time employee) by partially automating the close process to eliminate the need for double manual entry of branch accounts.*

Before:

- *Led numerous Kaizen events to dramatically improve production time and inventory turns.*

After:

- *Led 6–9 Kaizen blitz events and 80+ improvement projects yearly. In 4 years, reduced total production time from 50 days to 3 days and improved inventory turns from 4 to 11.*

Before:

- *Consistently met or exceeded monthly, quarterly, and yearly sales goals.*

After:

- Met or exceeded every sales goal for 4 straight years:

	2002	2003	2004	2005
Performance to Goal	125%	121%	101%	126%

Questions to Ask Yourself

Every position has specific expectations for performance. When you are considering your achievements and how best to present them, think about how your performance was evaluated and specific ways you were able to help the organization. These questions will help get your ideas flowing:

- Did I make money for the company? (Increase sales or other source of revenue?) If so, how much? How does that compare to what was expected of me? How does it compare to my peers or to industry averages?

- Did I save money? How much? How?

- Did I improve efficiency or productivity? How much? How?

- Did I save time? How much? How?

- Did I help the organization achieve a specific goal? What was it, what did I do, and what were the specific outcomes?

- Did I complete projects or assignments faster than expected?

- Did I solve a specific problem? What were the specific benefits that resulted?

- Did I attract new customers or retain existing customers? How many? How did it benefit the organization?

- What specific performance goals were established for me when I took the position or at the start of each year? How did I perform against those goals?

- Did I go "above and beyond" my job description to achieve something? If so, what was it, and what was the specific outcome?

15-MINUTE EXERCISE

Review your resume and see if you have written very specific, quantified achievements. If not, use the preceding questions to come up with three or four specific achievement statements for your most recent position. Then move backwards to earlier positions as time allows.

Most Recent Position

- _____
- _____
- _____
- _____

Next Most Recent Position

- _____
- _____
- _____
- _____

Next Most Recent Position

- _____
- _____
- _____
- _____

Quick Tips for Writing Achievement Statements

Here are a few tips for putting together effective achievement statements for your resume:

- As you move backward in time, as a general rule you can include less detail and fewer achievements for each position.

- Be sure that your achievement statements support your current goal. It is not necessary to write about everything you've done. For example, if you are a retail sales manager who wants a job in human resources, your achievement statements should relate to your HR-related successes in your job (perhaps recruiting, training, and motivating your staff), not your sales and merchandising activities.

- If you plan to write a functional- or skills-based resume rather than a chronological format, we suggest that you first organize the material by chronology and write achievement statements for each position. Then you can reorganize the most powerful and relevant achievements under functional headings.

Format for Readability, Impact, and Clarity

Good design not only improves the appearance of your resume, it makes your resume more readable, draws attention to the most important information, and guides the reader from one section to the next so that key information can be picked up in a quick skim.

With word-processing software, formatting options are endless. However, that doesn't mean you have to include an "endless" number of design elements or formatting enhancements in your resume. Keep in mind that your resume is a business document that should look professional. Readability, impact, and clarity are the key goals.

Here are a few quick formatting tips:

- **Use bold type to emphasize important information**—perhaps job titles, company names, numbers, and important achievements. Be careful not to use too much bold type, or you will reduce its effect.

- **Allow ample white space between sections of the resume.** White space lets the reader "breathe" before moving on to the next section.

- **Keep your paragraphs short** (three to five lines maximum). If a paragraph is too dense, it is uninviting to read and good information will be skipped over.

- **Keep your bullet lists short** (five to six items maximum). More than that, and the reader will absorb only the top few items and lose focus when moving down the long list.

- **Clearly distinguish one section of the resume from the next.** You might use large or different type for section headings or perhaps insert a horizontal rule (line) between sections.

- **Be consistent in how you format similar information.** For example, all of your job titles should be presented the same way, all company names should appear the same, section headers should be distinct from the rest of the resume but consistent for all headers, and so forth. When you are consistent, you provide clues to your reader about what kind of information you are presenting. It helps them read faster and understand more quickly.

- **Use a readable type size,** typically between 9 and 12 points for body copy. Some fonts (such as Verdana) are very readable at 9-point size, while others (such as Times New Roman) are quite small and rather hard to read at 10-point size. So adjust the point size in accordance with the fonts you use so your letter can be easily read.

Adapt Your Resume for Electronic Transmission

Because so much business correspondence takes place electronically, it is important that you be able to use your resume appropriately for e-mail, online applications, and other electronic methods. There are several different formats you can use, each with its advantages and limitations.

Microsoft Word

This is the standard word-processing format that is used by most businesses. It is important that you be able to send your resume in MS Word (.doc) format for easy opening and viewing by your recipients.

If you do not have Microsoft Word on your computer, you can try saving your file in Rich Text Format (.rtf). This kind of file can usually be opened by MS Word. Be sure you test this out by sending the RTF file to a friend who has Microsoft Word.

You can also visit your library or a local copy shop (such as FedEx Kinko's) where you can use the computer there and convert your resume to MS Word format. Then, save the file on a disk, bring it home, and send it as an attachment from your home computer.

PDF

Adobe's Portable Document Format (.pdf) is a helpful means of converting your file to a graphic that can easily be opened and read by anyone who downloads Adobe's free Acrobat Reader from www.adobe.com.

The advantage to this format is that your page layout remains intact and you don't have to worry about matching up word-processing programs with employers. A downside is that the graphic format is not "readable" as a text file into resume storage systems, and it is a little more awkward for recipients to deal with this format compared to the MS Word style they are likely accustomed to.

If you do not own the full version of Adobe Acrobat Distiller, you can access several sites on the Internet for free conversion of your resume to PDF format. A few we like are www.gobcl.com, www.k2pdf.com, and the Adobe site itself, https://createpdf.adobe.com/index.pl/. After converting your file, take the time to open and view it before sending it anywhere. Sometimes formatting glitches occur and you will have to make adjustments and reconvert the file.

Text-Only (ASCII)

Many Web sites require that you submit your resume as a text file without any formatting, boldfacing, or other design elements. This version, although plain and essentially unformatted, is entirely readable by any computer. In some instances, you might also want to include this text version of your resume (pasted into the body of your e-mail) when you are sending your MS Word version as an attachment.

You will need to follow a few simple steps to create the plain text version of your resume:

1. Create a new version of your resume using the "Save As" feature of your word-processing program. Select "text only," "ASCII," or "Plain Text (*.txt)" in the "Save As Type" option box.

2. Give a new name to this version and close the new file.

3. Reopen the file, and you'll find that your word processor has automatically reformatted your resume into Courier font, removed all formatting, and left-justified the text.

4. The removal of all formatting is likely to create some appearance problems that will need to be corrected. To promote maximum readability when sending your resume electronically, reset the margins to 2 inches left and right, so that you have a narrow column of text rather than a full-page width. (This margin setting will not be retained when you close the file, but in the meantime you can adjust the text formatting for best screen appearance. For instance, if you choose to include a horizontal line as suggested in step 8 [perhaps something like this: ++++++++++++++++++++++++++++] to separate sections of the resume, by working with the narrow margins you won't make the mistake of creating a line that extends past the normal screen width. Plus, you won't add hard line breaks that create odd-length lines when seen at normal screen width.)

5. Review the resume and fix any "glitches" such as odd characters that may have been inserted to take the place of "curly" quotes, dashes, accents, or other nonstandard symbols.

6. Remove any tabs and adjust spacing as necessary. You might add a few extra blank spaces at the beginning of a line or move text down to the next line.

7. If necessary, add extra blank lines to improve readability.

8. Consider adding horizontal dividers to break the resume into sections for improved skimmability. You can use a row of any standard typewriter symbols, such as *, -, (,), =, +, ^, or #.

When you close the file, it will be saved with the .txt file extension. When you are ready to use it, just open the file, select and copy the text, and paste it into your e-mail message or online application.

> ## 15-MINUTE EXERCISE
>
> Take a look at your resume. What do you want to stand out? Go through with a highlighter and mark those sections or words that you want to emphasize—the most important, most impressive information that is included in your resume. Then edit your resume onscreen, adding formatting enhancements as appropriate to emphasize the areas you highlighted. Be sure you have included only the most important information and that you have been consistent. When you are done, print the resume and review it again to be sure that the right information, and the right amount of information, is highlighted and now catches your attention. If you want to spend some more time, use the samples that follow to get some new ideas for ways to organize, highlight, and present information in your resume.

Sample Resumes

The 12 resumes that follow represent a broad variety of professions in diverse industries. But they follow all of our rules of resume writing. The objective is clear, accomplishments are highlighted, and each showcases a clean, effective design in which the important information stands out. Overall, the resumes are well organized and easy to skim for key information.

You can use these resumes to help you increase the readability, impact, and clarity of your resume—so that your resume will complement your cover letter and build on the positive impression you worked so hard to establish in your cover letters, e-mail follow ups, and initial phone calls.

Resume 1

Comments: For a maintenance mechanic who was a true "jack of all trades" and wanted to show the diversity of his skills and experience.

Matt Young
249 Maple Grove Road ▪ East Haven, CT 06512 ▪ 203-467-1276

MAINTENANCE MECHANIC

A true "handyman," mechanically inclined and extremely versatile, with more than 20 years of experience successfully handling a wide range of maintenance functions. Creative, quick, and resourceful in troubleshooting problems and finding solutions that minimize cost and downtime without sacrificing safety. Professional in workmanship and work ethic.

Areas of Experience

Mechanical Systems	Welding & Fabricating	Plant Maintenance
Gas Metal Arc Welding (Mig)	Hydraulics & Pumps	Plant Modifications
Electrical Mechanical Equipment	Pipefitting	Gas & Diesel Engines
Gear Drives & Chain Drives	Insulation	Railroad Equipment
Fleet Maintenance	Skid Loaders	Specialty Equipment

EXPERIENCE

Production Welder, 1/05–6/05 (temporary position)   Nutmeg Medical, New Haven, CT

- Completed 80-hour weld training program to meet stringent FDA requirements for the fabrication of healthcare equipment.
- Delivered high volume of top-quality work, welding 55 beds a day and averaging 15 seconds per weld.

Shop Foreman ▪ Mechanic ▪ Welder, 1995–2005   Short Line Construction, Branford, CT

- Managed projects and crew to keep railroad construction company fully productive and operating smoothly.
- Scheduled and managed maintenance for fleet of 11 vehicles, 23 pieces of small-engine equipment, 17 railroad apparatus, and a semi truck.
- Designed, fabricated, built, and modified equipment.
- Ordered parts and managed inventory.

Performance Highlights

- Quickly solved equipment breakdowns and emergencies, keeping downtime to a minimum.
- Dismantled and rebuilt tie-inserter machine, avoiding need for new purchase ($150K).
- Custom-built a truck to fit unusual demands of railroad equipment installation. Saved time and installation costs on every project thereafter.

Maintenance Mechanic, 1987–1995   Chem-Tech Industries, Inc., East Haven, CT

- Worked both independently and on team projects to keep chemical plant running smoothly, with minimal downtime and a low rate of preventable accidents.
- Involved in both routine maintenance and special projects such as motor replacements and pipe repairs that required production shut-down.

Journeyman, 1982–1987   Reinforced Concrete Ironworkers Local 459, New Haven, CT

- Worked on the construction and repair of major power plants along the East Coast.

EDUCATION / TRAINING / CERTIFICATION / LICENSE

- Basic Welding, Advanced Welding, Metallurgy—Connecticut Mechanical Institute, 2 years
- Local 459 Ironworker Apprenticeship—2 years Basic, 1 year Welding
- Certified in Welding for Aircraft Hardware (Titanium, Inconel, Hastelloy, Rene, etc.)
- Certified to weld Nuclear Stainless Steel
- Class B CDL (Commercial Driver's License)

Resume 2

Comments: For a new grad whose education is a primary qualification; his prior experience is included to show his work ethic and ability to take on new challenges.

Anthony T. LaMacchia

84 George Street, Apt. 6B, San Francisco, CA 94117   415-795-0094 — tonylama@aol.com

JOB TARGET	**Software Design / Programming / Testing / Technical Support**
QUALIFICATIONS	■ BS Computer Science ■ Technical curiosity; satisfaction in operating "behind the scenes" to make things work ■ Strong analytical, design, programming, and math skills ■ Teamwork experience and record of working effectively on both group and individual projects ■ Proven abilities to set and achieve goals, devise effective solutions, and defend opinions firmly and professionally
EDUCATION	BS Computer Science / Minor in Math 2005 University of California at Berkeley ■ Senior Design Project. With 3 teammates, created program to analyze blood samples for the University of California Medical School. ***Challenges:*** Open-ended design challenge called for abstract thinking, extensive pre-programming analysis, and team discussions to clarify approach and objectives before writing code.
COMPUTER SKILLS	■ Languages: C++, C, Java, Pascal ■ Software: Microsoft Word, Excel, Windows 98 and 2000 ■ Keyboarding: 85 wpm
LEADERSHIP QUALIFICATIONS	Selected for highly competitive Officer Candidate School, Quantico, VA. ■ ***Challenges:*** Completed math and technical academic testing, passing all components with grades of 80% or higher. Embarked on structured, rigorous fitness regimen to reach high level of physical fitness prior to entering demanding training program.
WORK EXPERIENCE	TDY Industries, San Mateo, CA Mill Operator (Summers 2003, 2004) ■ ***Challenges:*** Rapidly completed training to operate large equipment including forklift truck and recycling machinery for firm that recycles plastics into blasting materials for military and aircraft customers. Only employee (other than owners) entrusted to work alone on site, operating all equipment. Also worked in a cooperative team environment to promote efficiency and productivity. Road Builders, San Francisco, CA Field Technician (Summer 2002) ■ ***Challenges:*** As certified concrete tester, assessed quality of all freshly made concrete and made "go" or "no go" decisions that affected major construction projects. To ensure highest degree of quality and safety, stood my ground in enforcing quality decisions. Earned certification as ACI Concrete Field Testing Technician Grade I.

Resume 3

Comments: For a law-enforcement professional who wants to move from the sheriff's office to the police force of a large city.

Peter M. Quinn

7509 Maple Drive
East Haven, Connecticut 06555
203-467-8585   peterquinn@snet.net

Law Enforcement Officer

- Graduate of Connecticut Police Officer Training; certified 2003.
- Proven ability to deal effectively with prisoners, establishing respect for authority while treating individuals fairly.
- Thorough, hard working, disciplined, and reliable, with a serious attitude and a career commitment to law enforcement.

Professional Experience

NEW HAVEN COUNTY SHERIFF'S DEPARTMENT   2002–Present

Corrections Officer ▪ County Correctional Facility
Maintain inmate control over 100-plus prisoners in a dormitory-style jail. Supervise inmate behavior and respond to infractions. Count and lead prisoners to meals and recreation. Maintain detailed hourly logs and records of inmate transfers and other activities. Transport felons to higher-security jails. Assume responsibility in other areas of the jail on an occasional basis.

- Developed skills in dealing with individuals of all types.
- Gained experience in effectively handling tense situations.
- Consistently achieved excellent performance evaluations.
- Member of Sheriff's Power Lifting Team; hold an American record in bench press.

Other Experience

RYDER'S, New Haven, CT   2001–2002

Doorman/Bouncer

GRANT ASSOCIATES, New Haven, CT   1999–2001

Field Representative
Negotiated and sold the services of a collection firm to business clients such as mortgage companies, doctors, and other health-care providers.

Education

Connecticut Police Officer Training and Certification (2003), CONNECTICUT POLICE OFFICERS ACADEMY, Storrs, CT

Criminal Justice Degree Program (2002–Present), QUINNIPIAC COLLEGE, Hamden, CT

Graduate (1999), NORTH HAVEN HIGH SCHOOL, North Haven, CT
- Member of Wrestling Team

Resume 4

Comments: For a person who has performed both sales and service roles but wants to focus on client services.

Cynthia Evans

317-249-7590 Home ● 317-217-9076 Mobile ● evans@indy.rr.com
2594 West Allen Road, Indianapolis, IN 46218

PROFILE	**Client Services Professional**
Value Offered	• Record of top performance in demanding, high-volume customer-service roles. • Strengths in organization, time management, and the development of efficient processes. • Expert project management including meticulous note-taking and persistent follow-through. • Customer-service orientation and effective communications skills at all levels. • Impeccable record of attendance, timeliness, and dependability.
EXPERIENCE	**Midwest Health Partners,** Indianapolis, IN 2000–2005
	PROVIDER RELATIONS REPRESENTATIVE, 2002–2005: Promoted to sales/client services role, balancing cold-calling/outbound sales with attentive response to existing client inquiries. Tasked with expanding Midwest Health's network by securing contracts with medical groups, individual physicians, and hospital-based specialists. Efficiently scheduled and executed sales calls and marketing projects while managing a heavy load of daily inbound service calls.
Sales & Customer Service	• Consistently achieved customer-satisfaction scores in the high 90s. • Led the region in sales to hospital-based groups of specialty physicians—secured 10 new groups in 3 years.
Organization & Project Management	• Maintained detailed records of call history and created a foolproof follow-up system that ensured a consistent, persistent approach and led to excellent sales and service results. • Wrote sales letters and executed mass-mailings to target physicians. • Planned and coordinated meetings, events, and educational programs.
Presentation & Communication	• Represented Midwest Health at hospital-based health fairs. • Delivered informational presentations in the offices of newly contracted physicians; thoroughly explained the Midwest Health network and its operational procedures to ensure compliance and minimize problems.
	ADMINISTRATIVE ASSISTANT / OFFICE MANAGER, 2000–2002: Ensured smooth running of regional operation, managing all facets of office as well as a high volume of incoming calls.
Special Sales Assignments	• Personally handled special projects for the Regional Director, such as cold-calling clients for contract updates and executing mass mailings for physician marketing. Finished all projects on or ahead of schedule and with consistently high quality and accuracy. • Following merger, initiated hundreds of phone calls to introduce new doctors to Midwest Health and educate on policies/procedures.
	R.L. Stevens, Indianapolis, IN 1996–2000
	ADMINISTRATIVE ASSISTANT / WORD PROCESSOR: Provided expert word-processing support to 40–60 candidates in various stages of job transition.
Performance	• Consistently met or exceeded goal of 24-hour turnaround while client load *doubled*. • Twice nominated for Shining Star Award, the company's top performance award.
EDUCATION	Liberal Arts: Indiana University

Resume 5

Comments: For a mortgage professional who wants a job with less emphasis on selling and more on servicing loan accounts.

Casey Van Horn

513-791-1265   6843 Thoroughbred Trail, Cincinnati, OH 45239   cvanhorn@aol.com

MORTGAGE LOAN PROCESSOR

Experienced loan processor, office manager, and sales leader, repeatedly successful in achieving goals, completing challenging assignments, and managing processes and projects requiring close attention to detail and follow-through. Ten years of progressive experience and a record of solid performance when taking on new challenges and special assignments.

EXPERIENCE AND ACHIEVEMENTS

Mortgage Lenders of Ohio, Lebanon, OH   2003–Present

Processing/Office Manager

Manage fast pace of loan applications and office operations for branch of established mortgage firm. Interact extensively with clients both by telephone and face to face, gathering and recording personal and credit information to complete the loan application process. Schedule and attend closings.

- Accountable for timely submission of completed loan applications and supporting documents.
- Keep mortgage process on track and moving forward through heavy phone contact and persistent follow-up with attorneys, real estate agents, appraisers, and lenders.

Verizon Wireless, Cincinnati, OH   1995–2003

Manager, Indirect Accounts, 2002–2003

Managed relationships with 37 retail accounts statewide. Conducted in-store visits and training sessions to boost product knowledge, educate on sales strategies, and ensure the attainment of monthly sales goals.

- Established new Cash & Carry account with a national retailer. Involved in entire project including store build-out, product merchandising, and inventory procurement.
- Recognized as expert resource by retailers—repeatedly requested to assist with special events.
- Twice earned Retail Sales Award for top monthly performance.
- VIP Sales Award, 2002.

Telesales Manager, 2000–2002

Directed all activities of Telesales unit while continuing in full-time retail coordinator role. Managed 14 customer-service staff with a focus on efficiency and customer satisfaction. Created weekly staffing schedules; processed weekly payroll and exception reports.

- Collaborated with marketing team to plan and implement a successful outbound-calling campaign.
- Procured, installed, and implemented Telecheck system in the department.

Account Executive, 1995–2000

Provided inside-sales support for retail locations, including special sales campaigns and events.

- Consistently met or exceeded individual sales goals, ensuring group achievement of sales objectives.
- Earned recognition for "Extraordinary Customer Satisfaction."

EDUCATION & PROFESSIONAL DEVELOPMENT

AA degree in Business, Raymond Walters College (University of Cincinnati).

Ongoing training in management techniques, sales skills, new products, and computer use.

Resume 6

Comments: For a nurse with diverse experience; the list of skills and experience at the top shows broad capabilities.

Ann-Margaret O'Leary

2479 Oceanview Terrace, Miami, FL 33132 (305) 491-1010 • ann-margaret@hotmail.com

REGISTERED NURSE: Critical Care / Medical / Oncology

Dedicated, hard-working nurse with 7 years of diverse healthcare experience and recent nursing education/RN certification. Recognized by supervisors, peers, and professors for team orientation, high-level critical-thinking skills, and desire for continuous learning. Record of initiative in alerting healthcare team to changing patient status. Exceptional work ethic.

Hospital and clinic experience includes

• Monitoring vital signs	• Providing compassionate end-of-life care
• Administering EKGs and X rays	• Using cardiac monitors/interpreting cardiac rhythms
• Initiating oxygen therapy	• Drawing blood and initiating intravenous lines
• Caring for ventilated patients	• Assisting MDs with examinations and sterile procedures
• Bathing and tube-feeding	• Operating autoclave/conforming to sterilization protocols
• Administering injections	• Training new healthcare and administrative staff
• Educating patients and families	• Communicating patient information to healthcare team

HEALTHCARE EXPERIENCE

MEDICAL ASSISTANT: Hialeah Urgent Care and Family Clinic, Hialeah, FL   2002–Present
Serve a diverse patient population, beginning with triage and covering full range of urgent and ongoing care. Work cooperatively with physicians and other members of the healthcare team. Provide extensive patient education.
- Took on added responsibilities: taking X rays and EKGs, performing lab work, calling in medication renewals, and arranging consultations with specialists.
- Selected to train all new employees, identifying and filling in knowledge gaps to build overall staff capability.

PATIENT CARE ASSISTANT (CNA II): Miami-Dade Community Hospital, Miami, FL   2002–Present
On a combined medical/oncology unit, provide high level of care to patients—monitoring vital signs, bathing and tube-feeding patients, communicating patient status to the nursing team, and delivering end-of-life care with empathy and compassion.
- Recognized for ability to identify significant changes in status based on observation, intuition, and patient interaction.
- Effectively prioritized care during periods of staff shortages, dealing appropriately with patient concerns and complex medical issues.

CNA I, UNIT SECRETARY: South Florida Memorial Hospital, Miami, FL   2001–2002
Assisted nurses with care of critically ill patients on an emergency unit.
- Monitored cardiac monitors; interpreted rhythms; and notified nursing staff of changes in rhythm, oxygen saturation, respiratory rate, and blood pressure.
- As unit secretary, input physician orders into computer, answered phones, and paged physicians.

MEDICAL SPECIALIST: United States Army Reserves, Miami, FL   1996–2002
Provided preventative and emergency care including air and land evacuation of injured soldiers.
- Earned EMT certification.

EMERGENCY MEDICAL TECHNICIAN: Dade County Rescue Squad, Miami, FL   1999–2000

EDUCATION

Associate Degree in Nursing/RN Certification, May 2003
Miami-Dade Community College (NLN-accredited program), Miami, FL
- Held full-time nursing positions while carrying full course load.

Medical Specialist Course, 1998
Army Medical Department (AMEDD) Center and School, Ft. Sam Houston, TX

Fluent in Spanish. Proficient in a variety of computer applications.

Resume 7

Comments: For a marketing professional, this resume clearly emphasizes numbers, brand names, and results.

ROXANNE LOWE

617-823-4949   249 Marlborough Street, Boston, MA 02116   rolowe@attbi.com

MARKETING

PRODUCT MANAGEMENT ▶ **PRODUCT DEVELOPMENT** ▶ **PACKAGING**

Track record of revenue growth, profit enhancement, and successful product-line management during 9 years in progressively challenging marketing roles. Strong foundation in market research and technology paired with creativity and the ability to innovate. Talent for leading and inspiring teams to top performance.

- ▶ **Set new business directions** by recognizing and seizing market opportunities.
- ▶ **Improved performance in all products and brands managed;** grew revenues, cut costs, developed unique retailer programs and packages, and improved brand image.
- ▶ **Effectively prioritized multiple projects** to align results with business objectives.

EXPERIENCE

CORE CORPORATION, INC., Woburn, MA   1996–2005
($180M public company manufacturing and marketing consumer comfort products. Marquee brand is HappyFeet; key accounts include Wal-Mart, Federated, and other national retailers.)

SENIOR MARKETING MANAGER, 2002–2005—Led marketing strategy and programs for 3 product lines totaling $150M sales. Coordinated the efforts of design, product development, and manufacturing to deliver products for seasonal deadlines. Managed $2M marketing budget. Also directed the development of sales brochures and marketing materials; developed and gave sales-force presentations on seasonal product lines; and managed national sales meetings for upper management and national sales organization.

Increased sales and profitability in all 3 brand segments:

- ▶ **Value Brands:**
  - —Boosted profit margins from **25%** to **39%** through continuous improvement efforts that removed cost from every point of production—sourcing, production, packaging, distribution.
  - —Grew Wal-Mart program from **$3M** to **$7M** by identifying and capitalizing on sales trends.

- ▶ **HappyFeet™:**
  - —Created and launched Premier Collection, increasing total brand sales **60%** (**$5.8M** to **$9.3M**).
  - —Redesigned product displays to accommodate **20%** more product without increasing costs.

- ▶ **CoreComfort™:**
  - —Worked with manufacturing on technology-based line restage; product sales increased **31%**.
  - —Developed new packaging that increased inventory flexibility and saved **$95K** in first year.

PRODUCT MANAGER, 1998–2002—Recruited to join newly strengthened marketing team and challenged to improve performance of both private-label and branded products.

- ▶ Contributed to record sales performance, 1996: **$148M, 9%** growth over prior year.
- ▶ Developed POP sales program that increased retail space by more than **200%**.
- ▶ Spearheaded a packaging restage that generated **$8.1M** in incremental sales, reduced packaging costs **15%,** and improved packaging image and brand identification.

MARKETING ASSISTANT, 1996–1998

EDUCATION

MBA—Concentration: Marketing Management   Babson College, Wellesley, MA, 2002
BSBA—Concentration: Management   Boston College, Chestnut Hill, MA, 1996

Resume 8

Comments: For an accounting manager, this resume avoids repetitive lists of job duties and focuses on unique achievements.

Sean L. Thomas, CPA

7529 Beech Avenue, Naperville, IL 60564
(847) 555-1234 • seanthomas@yahoo.com

ACCOUNTING MANAGER / FINANCIAL ANALYST

Finance professional with a track record of cost savings and tight fiscal administration in both corporate and manufacturing environments. Verifiable accomplishments in corporate finance, plant accounting (both start-up and ongoing), and automated systems implementation.

Results-focused manager with proven ability to strategize, create project plans, implement, and follow through to completion. Effective communicator, skilled at gaining team support for key projects. Rapidly productive in new environments.

PROFESSIONAL EXPERIENCE

PLANET INDUSTRIES, INC., Detroit, Michigan, 1997–Present
Global manufacturer of plastic films, aluminum extrusions, and vinyl extrusions.

Accounting Manager, 2002–Present   *Plant Start-up, Evanston, Illinois*
Established all financial systems and controls for new manufacturing operation. Provided financial oversight during growth to $60 million in annual sales, with monthly operating budget of $700K.

- Spearheaded project to implement MRP II system. Oversaw in-house customization of software, system documentation, initial implementation and testing, and ongoing training to ensure active and appropriate use throughout the organization. Project completed on schedule and 5% under budget.

- Piloted an activity-based accounting program and prepared numerous cost/benefit analyses. Identified opportunities for increased efficiency and reduced operating costs, successfully quantifying criteria for capital projects.

Project Analyst, Fixed Assets, 1999–2002   *Corporate Headquarters, Detroit, Michigan*

- Implemented a fixed asset component to the company's mainframe system. Served as key project coordinator, tracking and documenting team activities to ensure successful completion— 3 weeks ahead of schedule, meeting all budget and performance parameters.

Staff Accountant, 1997–1999   *Corporate Headquarters, Detroit, Michigan*

- Performed cost accounting, budgeting, capital budget preparation, month-end closing, P&L statements, and full spectrum of corporate accounting functions.

PRIOR EXPERIENCE
- **Manager of Financial Reporting,** Concordia College, Ann Arbor, Michigan, 1995–1997
- **Fixed Asset Accountant,** GPA Packaging, Detroit, Michigan, 1994–1995
- **Cost / Budget Accountant,** Vinyl Corporation, Detroit, Michigan, 1991–1994

EDUCATION AND CERTIFICATION

B.S. Accounting, 1991: University of Michigan, Ann Arbor, Michigan
CPA certification, 1991

Resume 9

Comments: For a marketing and sales professional, this resume uses the challenge-action-results (CAR) format to tell relevant "success stories."

Maria Trujillo

29-A Primrose Court, Nashville, TN 37211
(615) 455-4555 • mjtrujillo@hotmail.com

MARKETING & SALES PROFESSIONAL

Out-of-the-box thinker who devises innovative marketing and sales strategies that deliver results in competitive markets. Expert in low-cost, high-ROI programs and fresh approaches to traditional projects. Well-organized and efficient manager who guides concepts to successful conclusion, with clear project plans and well-documented outcomes/results. Strong networker, relationship builder, and problem solver.

- B2B and B2C Marketing & Sales
- Dynamic Presentations
- Persistent Cold-Calling & Tenacious Follow-up
- Problem-Solving & Creative Workarounds
- Customer Relationship-Building

- Revenue & Profit Growth
- Contract Negotiations
- New Concept Introduction
- Benefits & Solution Selling
- Referral Network Development

PROFESSIONAL EXPERIENCE

Primrose Path Residential Community, Nashville, Tennessee   2002–Present

MANAGER   Focus on maintaining high occupancy rates through effective marketing and sales activities for residential apartment community for senior adults. In addition, manage day-to-day operations, supervise staff, and oversee facility maintenance.

Challenge   *Maintain occupancy in a niche market with constant attrition.*

Actions
- Through aggressive cold-calling and relationship development, established active referral network with professionals in health care and elderly services.
- Adapted sales presentation to focus on relevant features and benefits for individual audiences. Demonstrate strong customer orientation and excellent follow-through during lengthy, multi-step sales cycle.
- Increased response to advertising through new classification in rental-property publication; persistently pursued this idea to successful conclusion.

Results   **Reduced vacancy rate from 51% in 2002 to steadily maintained range of 1%–10% today. In first month on the job, conducted aggressive marketing campaigns that achieved occupancy for 90% of available units.**

OC Apartments, Nashville, Tennessee   1998–2002

MANAGER   Oversaw all aspects of day-to-day operations of 128-unit apartment complex occupied by university students. Recruited, trained, supervised, and scheduled 4 full-time employees.

Challenge   *Improve occupancy rate and stability of student-occupied complex; restore operating efficiency to poorly run facility.*

Actions
- Developed and implemented innovative marketing strategies to achieve goals for occupancy and stability. Created incentives for good grades and responsible occupancy; improved overall reputation of complex by increasing caliber of residents.
- Reorganized financial record-keeping, totally restructured the maintenance department, and tightly controlled and monitored expenses.

Results   **Improved occupancy from 80% to 100% within 5 months; consistently maintained high rate during tenure. Increased profitability by significantly reducing operating expenses.**

Resume 10

Comments: For a nightclub manager, this resume uses a bold format and functional headings to create eye appeal and draw attention to the most significant information.

FRANKIE DURAZO

Nightclub General Manager

Fifteen-year track record of leading world-class establishments that achieve:

- ☑ Consistent popularity
- ☑ Robust revenue and profit performance
- ☑ Exceptional safety records
- ☑ Strong revenue-security practices
- ☑ Positive community relationships
- ☑ Dedicated long-term staff

Extensive experience in all business, financial, and operational functions of high-volume clubs with diverse formats. Energetic and decisive leader. Motivational team builder. Organized and efficient manager. Effective communicator at all levels.

General Manager: Club Koko, Miami Beach, FL   1995–Present

Direct all business operations for world-renowned nightclub—a 15,000-sq.-ft. dance club with the world's top DJs and weekly revenues exceeding $100,000. On board since start-up, put in place the operating procedures, security standards, and revenue safeguards that have been pivotal to long-term success and profitable operation of the club.

Recruit, train, and manage 42 staff. Manage financial operations including monthly budgets, payroll, assessments, and inventory. Ensure compliance with all building and safety codes; oversee building maintenance including A/C, plumbing, and electrical. Remain highly visible on the floor and personally handle all VIPs.

- ☑ **Site selection & construction:** Assisted owners in locating and selecting site in up-and-coming South Beach neighborhood. Oversaw building construction and club layout. Represented owners at community meetings and before licensing boards.

- ☑ **Revenue protection:** Established foolproof ticketing system that eliminates non-paying guests and guarantees revenue accountability. Set demanding standards for door staff and hold them accountable.

- ☑ **Guest safety & security:** Created effective security system that minimizes use of illegal substances and promotes a safe environment—since launched, zero incidents. In demand as consultant to introduce similar systems in other New York clubs.

- ☑ **Community relations:** Instituted street-side crowd control to minimize neighborhood disturbances. Personally visible and accessible to all neighbors.

- ☑ **Special events:** Oversee highly profitable special events entailing club rental, custom decorating, and catering. Steadily grew special-event revenue 20% or more each year.

- ☑ **City agency relations:** Personally secured and maintained up-to-date city licenses for fire safety and building security. Built excellent relationships with City of Miami Fire and Police Departments.

- ☑ **Staff loyalty & reliability:** In high-turnover industry, retained staff long term—including 5 bar staff and 2 coat-check staff since opening of club. Constantly improve staff skills through training. Create a positive, team-oriented culture.

Mobile: 305-209-8003   2532 Flamingo Lane, Coral Gables, FL 33146   **FDurazo@hotmail.com**

Resume 11

Comments: For an operations manager who has several stellar career achievements that are highlighted front and center.

Paul Fontaine

(513) 555-0808   4725 Kemp Grove Road
pfontaine@fuse.net   Loveland, OH 45140

Expertise: Technology Services Operations Management

**Strategic Analysis and Planning — Management — Performance Improvements
Marketing & Sales — Staff Development**

Career Highlights

- Led across-the-board operational improvements that helped a computer company to grow 35% per year, outperforming aggressive goals and successfully positioning the company for acquisition. Retained as Operations Director following buy-out.

- Developed service and customer focus as strong competitive advantages. Motivated staff and successfully instilled a strong client-first orientation in sales and service teams.

- Juggled multiple challenges while maintaining peak performance. E.g., completed MBA while working full time; took on added consulting position while employed by American Candy. Consistently used exceptional multitasking skills to maintain a high level of personal productivity.

Professional Experience

TECHNO-SOLUTIONS, INC., Cincinnati, Ohio   1999–Present
Full-service computer solutions firm; purchased by Xy-Tech in 2004 for $52 million

Operations Director, 2000–Present

Direct all activities for rapidly growing computer services firm offering hardware, software, and network solutions to Fortune 100 clients. Accountable for sales, profitability, customer satisfaction, and all aspects of operations (inventory, purchasing, shipping & receiving), overseeing 12 direct and 60 indirect reports.

Develop and implement strategic plans to achieve corporate goals for growth and profitability.

- Increased sales 35% annually, outperforming goal of 30%.

- Improved company-wide skill levels, morale, and teamwork through training, judicious hiring, and weeding out under-performing staff. Developed expert technical staff as a competitive advantage.

- Promoted company image as customer problem-solver able to deliver both long-range solutions and "fast fixes" for immediate productivity.

- Slashed product delivery time from 4 days to 1–2 days by realigning staff schedules and communicating urgency to vendors.

- Created and implemented aggressive sales, marketing, and advertising campaign targeting our key audience, MIS professionals.

- Consistently delivered excellent quality, value, and service, to the point where volume of referral business eliminated the need for costly advertising.

Management / Operations Consultant, 1999–2000

Challenged to develop operational improvements to deliver 30% annual growth. Analyzed entire operating structure; identified opportunities for significant improvement in customer service and business development.

- Offered permanent position as Operations Director as a result of findings and contributions during consulting assignment.

Resume 12

Comments: For a senior executive, hard numbers and results are emphasized with enough detail to explain how they were achieved.

Dana T. Singer

dtsinger@austin.rr.com

7551 Texas Trail
Austin, TX 78728
Home: 512-555-8345
Office: 512-555-0904

Senior Management Executive

Driving Strategic, Profitable Growth for Start-up to Fortune 500 Organizations

Creative business strategist with a strong record of career achievements that include
— Leading fast-growth start-ups
— Revitalizing flagging operations
— Delivering strong and sustained revenue growth
— Consolidating and cost-cutting to improve profit performance
— Repositioning sales strategies for long-term growth

Multimillion-dollar P&L responsibility for Fortune 500 and early-stage companies with U.S. and international operations. Extensive M&A experience, from assessment through integration. History of identifying and capturing beneficial strategic partnerships.

Unquestionable integrity and total commitment to providing outstanding customer service and creating value for shareholders.

Experience and Accomplishments

Safety Software (Subsidiary of Software Central, Inc.), Austin, TX   2003–Present

World's largest provider of public-safety software and consulting services—$500M revenue, 12 global locations

PRESIDENT

Brought on board to spearhead rapid, profitable growth—to create and execute growth strategies, develop a strong management team, acquire and integrate complementary businesses, negotiate strategic alliances, and drive sales/business development. Manage P&L, operations, and sales. Directly manage 4 VPs who oversee 400 employees in the U.S., Europe, and Asia.

- Grew revenues from $120M to $500M through acquisition and organic growth.
- Increased EBITDA from 10% to 17% through consolidation strategies.
- Spearheaded active acquisition drive and managed due diligence, negotiations, and integration for 5 acquisitions in 2 years.
- Retained experienced, entrepreneurial managers in each location, successfully renewing management contracts of more than 80% of original business owners into second year of Safety Software ownership.
- Vigorously pursued strategic partnerships to build visibility, support the development of complementary products and services, and firmly position Safety as the industry leader. Partners include
  — Manufacturers of handheld and in-vehicle data terminals
  — Professional associations within the law-enforcement and fire-prevention fields
  — Leading online training companies specializing in public-safety training
  — Major Web portals with high visibility and credibility in the public-safety industry

CORPORATE VICE PRESIDENT, SOFTWARE CENTRAL, INC. (concurrent role)

Participate in strategy and business planning as a member of the executive team of Software Central, a fast-growing $200M conglomerate of niche software providers.

- Instrumental in acquisition of P-Plus, the market-share leader in PDA peripherals.
- Leveraged Safety Software's law enforcement expertise to position Software Central for growth opportunity in public-safety database enhancement.

Key Points: Chapter 5

Here are the key points of this chapter:

- Many resumes lack power and effectiveness because of a few key problem areas:
    - Clarity
    - Focus
    - Relevance
    - Appearance
- You can quickly improve your resume by evaluating these areas and editing, organizing, and formatting to be sure that:
    1. Your objective is crystal clear.
    2. You have highlighted your unique achievements.
    3. Your format promotes readability, impact, and clarity.
- Sample resumes provided in this chapter will give you good ideas for content, style, design, and overall presentation that you can adapt for your own unique resume.

Chapter 6

Seven Steps to Getting a Good Job in Less Time

This chapter is designed to provide you with an overview of career planning and job seeking skills. It illustrates quick but helpful techniques you can use to shorten the time it takes to get a job.

You might have jumped to this chapter right away, or after quickly reviewing the strategies we suggest for quick yet effective cover letters and resumes. We hope that is the case because the value of your resume and cover letter is in what they will help you accomplish—which is getting a good job.

The Quick Job Search: Career Planning and Job Search Advice

We have found that few books on resumes and cover letters provide good advice on job seeking. In fact, most of these books give bad advice. For example, they often tell you to send out lots of resumes and get them onto employers' desks or into e-mail boxes or resume-scanning systems. Then, if your resume or cover letter is good enough, employers will ask you in for an interview.

> **Note:** *If you are planning your career or need to know more about finding a job, we strongly encourage you to learn more. Another book by one of the authors, Michael Farr, titled* The Very Quick Job Search, *covers the techniques in this section in much greater depth and provides other information as well. It is published by JIST and is available through most bookstores and libraries.*

This advice is old-fashioned and downright harmful. It puts you at the mercy of some employer whose mindset is to screen people out. It encourages you to be passive and wait for employers to call you. And, worst of all, it assumes that the job search is limited to talking to employers who have job openings now and excludes all those who do not—but who might soon.

So we think the traditional advice on resumes and job seeking is (to put it kindly) not good. You can use techniques that are far more effective than the traditional ones. Over many years, we have found that the best job search techniques are based on common sense. They encourage you to be clear about what you want and then to go out and actively look for it. It takes some nerve, but people who use the techniques presented in this chapter have proven that they do work. The techniques will help you find better jobs in less time. And that is what a job search should be all about, isn't it?

Two Very Important Points About Job Search Methods

We want to make two points that apply to the Internet as well as to other job search methods:

1. **It is unwise to rely on just one or two job search methods.** You should use every option available to you, including networking and responding to job postings online and off.

2. **It is essential that you take an active rather than a passive approach in your job search.** You can't sit back and wait for employers to call you. You must talk to people and find the jobs.

Avoid the Temptation to Just Scan This Material—Do the Activities

We know that you will resist doing the activities included here. But trust us: Completing them is worthwhile. Those who do them will have a better sense of what they are good at, what they want to do, and how to go about doing it. They are likely to get more interviews and to present themselves better in those interviews. Is this worth giving up a night of TV? Yes, we think so.

Interestingly, you will—after reading this chapter and doing its activities—have spent more time planning your career than most people. You will know far more than the average job seeker about how to go about finding a job. Although you may want to know more, what you learn here is enough to get you started.

This book will teach you techniques to find a better job in less time. But job seeking requires you to act, not just learn. So consider what you can do to put the techniques to work for you. Do the activities. Create a daily plan. Get more interviews—today, not tomorrow. You see, the sooner and harder you get to work on your job search, the shorter it is likely to be.

Changing Jobs and Careers Is Often Healthy

Most of us were told from an early age that each career move must be up, involving more money, responsibility, and prestige. However, research indicates that people change careers for many other reasons as well.

In a survey conducted by the Gallup Organization for the National Occupational Information Coordinating Committee, 44 percent of the working adults surveyed expected to be in a different job within three years. Yet only 41 percent had a definite plan to follow in mapping out their careers.

Logical, ordered careers are found more often with increasing levels of education. But you should not assume this means that occupational stability is healthy. Many adult developmental psychologists believe occupational change is not only normal, but may even be necessary for sound adult growth and development.

It is common, even normal, to reconsider occupational roles during your twenties, thirties, and forties, even in the absence of economic pressure to do so. One viewpoint is that a healthy occupational change allows some previously undeveloped aspect of the self to emerge. The change may be as natural as from clerk to supervisor or as drastic as from professional musician to airline pilot. Although risk is always a factor when change is involved, reasonable risks are healthy and can raise self-esteem.

Whether you are seeking similar work in another setting or changing careers, you need a workable plan to find the right job. The rest of this chapter gives you the information you need to help you find a good job quickly. Short as this chapter is, it does present you with the basic skills to find a good job in less time. The techniques work.

Seven Steps for a Quick and Successful Job Search

You can't just read about getting a job. The best way to get a job is to go out and get interviews! The best way to get interviews is to make a job out of getting a job. We have identified just seven things you need to do that make a big difference in your job search. The following sections cover each of these steps.

Seven Steps for a Quick Job Search

1. Identify your skills.
2. Have a clear job objective.
3. Know where and how to look for job leads.
4. Spend at least 25 hours a week looking for a job—more if you're currently unemployed.
5. Get two interviews a day.
6. Do well in interviews.
7. Follow up on all contacts.

Step 1: Identify Your Skills

An effective career plan requires that you know your skills. If you have not spent time on this issue, we strongly suggest that you do. It is very important for both planning your career and for presenting yourself effectively throughout the job search.

Most job seekers cannot answer the question, "Why should I hire you?" The consequence of not being able to answer that question, as you might guess, is that your chances of getting a job offer are greatly reduced. Knowing your skills, therefore, gives you a distinct advantage in the job search, helps you write a more effective resume, and helps you focus your cover letters on the most relevant information.

A useful way to organize skills is to divide them into three basic types: Adaptive skills (personality traits), transferable skills, and job-related skills.

- **Adaptive skills (personality traits)** are the skills you use every day to survive and get along. They allow you to adapt or adjust to a variety of situations. Some of them also could be considered part of your basic personality. Examples of adaptive skills valued by employers include getting to work on time, honesty, enthusiasm, and getting along with others.

- **Transferable skills** are general skills that can be used in a variety of jobs. For example, writing clearly, good language skills, and the ability to organize and prioritize tasks would be desirable skills in many jobs. These are called transferable skills because they can be transferred from one job—or even one career—to another.

- **Job-related skills** are what people typically first think of when asked, "Do you have any skills?" These skills are related to a particular job or type of work. An auto mechanic, for example, needs to know how to tune engines and repair brakes. An accountant needs to know how to create a general ledger, use computerized accounting programs, and perform other activities related to that job.

YOUR SKILLS SUMMARY

List your top five adaptive/self-management skills:

1. _____
2. _____
3. _____
4. _____
5. _____

List your top five transferable skills:

1. _____
2. _____
3. _____
4. _____
5. _____

(continued)

(continued)

List your top five job-related skills:

1. _____

2. _____

3. _____

4. _____

5. _____

If you wish to delve further into this topic, you can find in-depth information on identifying your skills in several good books, including Mike Farr's *The Quick Resume & Cover Letter Book* and *The Very Quick Job Search*. These are widely available in libraries and bookstores.

The Skills Employers Want Most

When evaluating your skill set, consider these skills that employers want most, according to a study conducted by the U.S. Department of Labor and the American Association of Counseling and Development:

1. Learning to learn
2. Basic academic skills in reading, writing, and computation
3. Listening and oral communication
4. Creative thinking and problem solving
5. Self-esteem and goal setting
6. Personal and career development
7. Interpersonal skills
8. Negotiation and teamwork
9. Organizational effectiveness and leadership

Step 2: Have a Clear Job Objective

Having a clear job objective is not just an issue for your cover letters and resume. We realize how difficult it can be to figure out the exact job you want; however, getting as close as you can is essential.

Too many people look for a job without having a good idea of exactly what they are looking for. Before you go out looking for "a" job, we suggest that you first define exactly what it is you really want—"the" job. Most people think a job objective is the same as a job title, but it isn't. You need to consider other elements of what makes a job satisfying for you. Then, later, you can decide what that job is called and what industry it might be in.

Here are a few points to summarize the elements to consider in your ideal job.

YOUR IDEAL JOB

What skills do you want to use?

1. _____

2. _____

3. _____

4. _____

5. _____

What special knowledge would you like to use in your ideal job?

_____

_____

_____

What types of people do you like to work with or for? _____

_____

_____

_____

What type of work environment do you prefer? _____

_____

_____

_____

(continued)

(continued)

Where do you want your next job to be located? _____

_____

_____

_____

How much money do you hope to make in your next job? _____

_____

How much responsibility are you willing to accept? _____

_____

_____

_____

What things are important or have meaning to you?_____

_____

_____

_____

Describe your ideal job:_____

_____

_____

_____

Step 3: Know Where and How to Look for Job Leads

One survey found that about 85 percent of all employers don't advertise their job openings. They hire people they know, people who find out about the jobs through word of mouth, or people who happen to be in the right place at the right time. While the Internet has changed how some employers find people, getting a solid lead is still too often a matter of "luck." But the good news is that, by using the right techniques, you can learn to increase your "luck" in finding job openings.

Traditional Job Search Methods Are Not Very Effective

Most job seekers don't know how ineffective some traditional job hunting techniques tend to be. For example, a recent *New York Times* survey showed that fewer than 15 percent of all job seekers get jobs from responding to want ads and online job postings.

Here is more detail on the effectiveness of seven of the most popular traditional job search methods:

- **Help-wanted ads and online postings:** Less than 15 percent of all people get their jobs through advertised openings. Everyone who reads the paper or visits the job sites knows about these openings, so competition for advertised jobs is fierce. Still, some people get jobs through ads, so go ahead and apply. Just be sure to spend most of your time using more effective methods.

- **State employment services:** Each state has a network of local offices to administer unemployment compensation and provide job leads and other services. These services are provided without charge to you or employers. Names of these offices vary by state, so your local office may be called "Job Service," "Department of Labor," "Workforce Development," "Unemployment Office," or another name.

  Nationally, only about 5 percent of all job seekers get their jobs here, and these organizations typically know of only one-tenth (or fewer) of the job openings in a region. Local openings are posted on a government-funded Internet site at www.ajb.dni.gov, where you can search by occupation and location anywhere in the country.

- **Private employment agencies:** Recent studies have found that staffing agencies work reasonably well for those who use them. But consider some cautions. For one thing, these agencies work best for entry-level positions or for those with specialized, in-demand skills. Most people who use a private agency usually

> **Tip:** *Never work with a search firm or employment agency that charges you to get a job through them. Legitimate firms are paid only by the employer for whom they fill jobs. There should be no cost to you. (But don't confuse this advice with the fees you pay to private-practice career counselors or coaches; they provide coaching services for a fee and don't promise you a job.)*

find their jobs using some other source, making the success record of these businesses quite modest.

Private agencies charge a fee as high as 20 percent of your annual salary to you or to the employer. Because of the high expense, you can require that you be referred only to interviews where the employer pays the fee. Keep in mind that most private agencies find job openings by calling employers, something you could do yourself.

- **Temporary agencies:** These can be a source of quick but temporary jobs to bring in some income while you look for long-term employment. Temp jobs also give you experience in a variety of settings— something that can help you land full-time jobs later. More and more employers are also using these jobs as a way to evaluate workers for permanent jobs. So consider using these agencies if it makes sense, but continue an active search for a full-time job.

- **Sending out resumes:** One survey found that you would have to mail more than 500 unsolicited resumes to get one interview! Like other traditional approaches, use this method sparingly because the numbers are stacked against you.

  A better approach is to contact the person who might hire you, by phone or via e-mail, to set up an interview directly—then send a cover letter and resume. If you insist on sending out unsolicited resumes, do this on weekends and evenings and save your "prime time" for more effective job search techniques.

- **Filling out applications:** Most applications are used to screen you out. Larger organizations may require them, but remember that your task is to get an interview, not fill out an application. If you do complete applications, make them neat and error-free and do not include anything that could get you

  > **Tip:** If necessary, leave a problem question or section blank on an application. You can always explain it after you get an interview.

  screened out. Never present something in a way an employer would see as a negative. For example, instead of saying you were "fired," say "position eliminated due to corporate downsizing." If the form asks for pay requirements, simply write in something like "flexible" instead of giving a specific number.

- **Human resource departments:** Hardly anyone gets hired by interviewers in HR or personnel departments. Their job is to screen you and then refer the "best" applicants to the person who would supervise you. You may need to cooperate with the people in HR, but it is often better to go directly to the person who is most likely to supervise you—even if no opening exists at the moment. And remember that many smaller organizations don't even have HR or personnel offices.

The Two Job Search Methods That Work Best: Warm and Cold Contacts

About two-thirds of all people get their jobs using informal methods. These jobs are often not advertised and are part of the "hidden" job market. How can you find them?

There are two basic informal job search methods: networking with people you know (which we call warm contacts), and making direct contacts with employers (which we call cold contacts). They are both based on the most important job search rule of all:

The Most Important Job Search Rule:
Don't wait until the job is open before contacting the employer!

Most jobs are filled by someone the employer meets before the job is formally open. So the trick is to meet people who can hire you *before* a job is available! Instead of saying, "Do you have any jobs open?" say, "I realize you may not have any openings now, but I would still like to talk to you about the possibility of future openings."

Develop a Network of Contacts in Five Easy Steps

One study found that about 40 percent of all people found their jobs through a lead provided by a friend, a relative, or an acquaintance. Developing new contacts is called "networking," and here's how it works:

1. **Make lists of people you know.** Develop a list of anyone with whom you are friendly; then make a separate list of all your relatives. These two lists alone often add up to 25 to 100 people or more. Next, think of other groups with whom you have something in common, such as former coworkers or classmates, members of your social or sports

groups, members of your professional association, former employers, and members of your religious group. You may not know many of these people personally, but most will help you if you ask them.

2. **Contact the people on your lists in a systematic way.** Each of these people is a contact for you. Obviously, some lists and some people on those lists will be more helpful than others, but almost any one of them could help you find a job lead.

3. **Present yourself well.** Begin with your friends and relatives. Call or e-mail them and tell them you are looking for a job and need their help. Be as clear as possible about what you are looking for and what skills and qualifications you have. Look at the sample phone script later in this chapter for presentation ideas.

4. **Ask them for leads.** It is possible that they will know of a job opening that is just right for you. If so, get the details and get right on it! More likely, however, they will not, so ask them the Three Magic Networking Questions in the following sidebar:

The Three Magic Networking Questions

1. **Do you know of any openings for a person with my skills?** If the answer is no (which it usually is), ask the next question.

2. **Do you know of someone else who might know of such an opening?** If your contact does, get that name and ask for another one. If he or she doesn't, ask the next question.

3. **Do you know of anyone who might know of someone else who might?** Another good way to ask this is "Do you know someone who knows lots of people?" If all else fails, this will usually get you a name.

---

5. **Contact these referrals and ask them the same questions.** For each original contact, you can extend your network of acquaintances by hundreds of people. Eventually, one of these people will hire you or refer you to someone who will! If you use networking thoroughly, it may be the only job search technique you'll need.

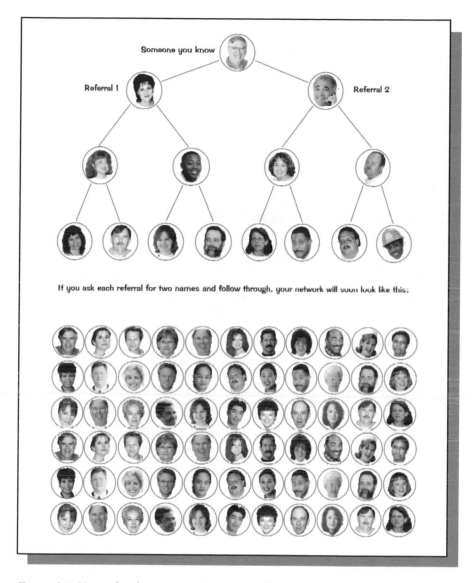

Figure 6-1: How referrals can expand your network.

If you're worried that you don't know enough people to network effectively, concentrate on going to group events where you'll have a large pool of people from which to develop contacts, rather than just meeting people one by one. Attend professional association meetings, lectures, classes, social functions, and anywhere that you can meet a lot of folks.

Networking is about much more than asking people if they know of any job openings. The answer is likely to be no, so that question doesn't get you far. Instead, look at networking as a way to build relationships with people who know other people, who may know other people who know of jobs. Networking is also about getting advice about your search and insight into the organizations you're trying to break into.

> **Note:** *For much more advice about this important topic of networking and how to make it work for you, we recommend reading* Networking for Job Search and Career Success *by Michelle Tullier (JIST Publishing).*

Use Cold Contacts—Contact Employers Directly

It takes more courage, but contacting an employer directly is a variation on the networking idea and a very effective job search technique. We call these "cold contacts" because you don't know or have an existing connection with the employers. Following are three basic techniques for making cold contacts:

- **Use the *Yellow Pages* to find potential employers.** Online sites like www.yellowpages.com and others allow you to find potential employers anywhere, but the print version is best if you're looking for a local job. You can begin by looking at the index and asking for each entry, "Would an organization of this kind need a person with my skills?" If the answer is "yes," then that type of organization or business is a possible target. You can also rate "yes" entries based on your interest, writing an "A" next to those that seem very interesting, a "B" next to those you are not sure of, and a "C" next to those that don't seem interesting at all.

  Next, select a type of organization that got a "yes" response (such as "hotels") and turn to the section of the *Yellow Pages* where they are listed. Then call the organizations and ask to speak to the person who is most likely to hire or supervise you. A sample telephone script is included on the following page to give you ideas about what to say.

  The Internet provides a variety of ways to do the same thing. For example, *Yellow Pages* listings are available online for any geographic area of the country. And many businesses have Web sites where you can get information and apply for job openings.

  Another good source of company information is your city's business journal, where you will typically find annual reports of the city's top

100 businesses in a specific industry or area. Your Chamber of Commerce can provide additional information, and the reference librarian at your local library can be a gold mine of information about how to find companies that might be able to use someone with your skills.

- **Drop in without an appointment.** Although building security has become increasingly tight in some locations, you can sometimes simply walk into many potential employers' organizations and ask to speak to the person in charge. This is particularly effective in small businesses, but it works surprisingly well in larger ones, too. Remember, you want an interview even if there are no openings now. If your timing is inconvenient, ask for a better time to come back for an interview.

While this method can be effective, it can be very time-consuming depending on travel distances and how closely grouped your target companies are. Use this method occasionally to get yourself out and about and into new areas. The variety is likely to energize other aspects of your search.

- **Use the phone to get job leads.** Once you have created your JIST Card (see chapter 4), it is easy to create a telephone contact script based on it. Adapt the basic script to call people you know or your *Yellow Pages* leads. Select *Yellow Pages* index categories that might use a person with your skills and get the numbers of specific organizations in that category. Once you get to the person who is most likely to supervise you, present your phone script.

Although it doesn't work every time, most people, with practice, can get one or more interviews in an hour by making these cold calls. Here is a sample phone script based on a JIST Card:

> *Hello, my name is Pam Nykanen. I'm interested in a position in hotel management. I have four years of experience in sales, catering, and accounting with a 300-room hotel. I also have an associate degree in Hotel Management plus one year of experience with the Bradey Culinary Institute. During my employment, I helped double revenues from meetings and conferences and increased bar revenues by 46 percent. I have excellent problem-solving skills and am good with people. I am also well organized, hardworking, and detail oriented. When may I come in for an interview?*

Note that this script is clear, concise, and focuses on what you know (your experience) and what you have done (your accomplishments). In a capsule form, you have given the hiring manager enough information to know whether he or she is likely to need someone like you, either immediately or in the near future.

Resist the temptation to share your entire background and all of your qualifications and achievements. Your goal is to pique the interest of your audience and transform your monologue to a dialogue.

This example assumes that you are calling someone you don't know; however, the script can be easily modified for presentation to warm contacts, including referrals. Using the script for making cold calls takes courage, but it works for most people.

Most Jobs Are with Small Employers

About 70 percent of all people work in small businesses—those with 250 or fewer employees. While the largest corporations have reduced the number of employees, small businesses have been creating as many as 80 percent of the new jobs over the past decade.

Smaller organizations are where most of the job search action is, so do not ignore this fact. Many opportunities exist to obtain training and promotions in smaller organizations, too. Many do not even have HR departments, so nontraditional job search techniques are particularly effective with them.

Step 4: Spend 25 Hours or More a Week Looking for a Job

On the average, job seekers spend fewer than 15 hours a week looking for work. The average length of unemployment varies from three or more months, with some being out of work far longer (older workers and higher earners are two groups who take longer). There is a clear connection between how long it takes to find a job and the number of hours spent looking on a daily and weekly basis.

Based on many years of experience, we can say that the more time you spend on your job search each week, the less time you are likely to remain unemployed. Of course, using more effective job search methods also helps. Those who follow this advice have proven, over and over, that they get jobs in less than half the average time; and they often get better jobs, too. Time management is the key.

If you are unemployed and looking for a full-time job, you should look for a job on a full-time basis. It just makes sense, although many do not do so because of discouragement, lack of good techniques, and lack of structure. Most job seekers have no idea what they are going to do next Thursday—they don't have a plan. The most important thing is to decide how many hours you can commit to your job search, and stay with it. If you are unemployed, you should spend a minimum of 25

> **Tip:** *Of course, if you are currently employed and looking for a better job, you will spend less than 25 hours a week looking—but the principles remain the same.*

hours a week on hard-core job search activities with no goofing around, and even more time is better. The following worksheet walks you through a simple but effective process to help you organize your job search schedule.

STRUCTURE YOUR JOB SEARCH LIKE A JOB

1. **Decide how many hours you will spend a week looking for work.**

   Write here how many hours you are willing to spend each week looking for a job: _____

2. **Decide which days and times you will look for work.**

   Answering the following questions requires you to have a schedule and a plan, just as you had when you were working.

   Which days of the week will you spend looking for a job? _____

   _____

   How many hours will you look each day? _____

   At what time will you begin and end your job search on each of these days? _____

3. **Create a specific daily schedule.**

   A specific daily job search schedule is very important because most job seekers find it hard to stay productive each day. You already know which job search methods are most effective, and you should plan on spending most of your time using those methods.

(continued)

(continued)

The sample daily schedule that follows has been very effective for people who have used it, and it will give you ideas for your own. Although you are welcome to create your daily schedule however you like, we urge you to consider one similar to this one. Why? Because it works.

7–8 a.m.	Get up, shower, dress, eat breakfast.
8–8:15 a.m.	Organize work space; review schedule for interviews or follow-ups; update schedule.
8:15–9 a.m.	Review old leads for follow-up; develop new leads (want ads, Internet, networking lists, and so on).
9–10 a.m.	Make networking or direct employer phone calls or Internet contacts; set up meetings and interviews.
10–10:15 a.m.	Take a break!
10:15–11 a.m.	Make more new calls and Internet contacts.
11–12 p.m.	Make follow-up calls and e-mails as needed.
12–1 p.m.	Lunch break.
1–5 p.m.	Go on interviews and networking meetings; make cold contacts in the field; conduct research for upcoming interviews.
5–8 p.m.	Attend networking events.

4. **Get a schedule book and write down your job search schedule.**

   This is important: If you are not accustomed to using a daily schedule book, PDA, or planner, promise yourself that you will get a good one today. Choose one that allows plenty of space for each day's plan on an hourly basis, plus room for daily "to-do" listings. Write in your daily schedule in advance; then add interviews as they come. Get used to carrying it with you and using it!

Step 5: Get Two Interviews a Day

The average job seeker gets about five interviews a month—fewer than two interviews a week. Yet many job seekers using the techniques we suggest routinely get two interviews a day. But to accomplish this, you must first redefine what an interview is (see below).

With this definition, it is *much* easier to get interviews. You can now interview with all kinds of potential employers, not just those who have job openings. Many job seekers use the *Yellow Pages* to get two interviews with just one hour of calls by using the telephone contact script discussed earlier. Others drop in on a potential employer and ask for an unscheduled interview—and they get one. And getting names of others to contact from those you know—networking—is extremely effective if you persist.

> **Tip:** *Getting two interviews a day equals 10 a week and 40 a month. That's 800 percent more interviews than the average job seeker gets. Who do you think will get a job offer quicker? So set out each day to get at least two interviews. It's quite possible to do, now that you know how.*

The New Definition of an Interview

An interview is any face to face contact with a person who has the authority to hire or supervise someone with your skills. The person may or may not have an opening at the time.

Step 6: Do Well in Interviews

No matter how you get an interview, once you are there, you will have to create a good impression…

- Even if your resume is one of the 10 best ever written.

- Even if you have the best of credentials.

- Even if you really want the job.

> **Tip:** *One study indicated that, of those who made it as far as the interview (many others were screened out before then), about 40 percent created a bad first impression, mostly based on their dress and grooming. First impressions count, and if you make a bad one, your chances of getting a job offer rapidly decrease to about zero.*

Dress for Success

Although there is more to making a good first impression than your dress and grooming, this is fortunately something that you can change readily. So, for this reason, Mike Farr created the following rule (and, we point out, this is one of the very few rules you will see in this book):

> ### *Farr's Dress and Grooming Rule:*
> Dress the way you think the boss is most likely to dress—only neater.

Dress for success. If necessary, ask someone who dresses well to help you select an interview outfit. Pay close attention to your grooming, too.

Tough Interview Questions

Interviews are where the job search action happens. You have to get them; then you have to do well in them. If you have done your homework, you will seek out interviews for jobs that will maximize your skills. That is a good start, but your ability to communicate your skills in the interview makes an enormous difference.

> **Tip:** *Your written materials such as cover letters and resumes must be neat and error-free as well, since they also create a first impression.*

This is where, according to employer surveys, most job seekers have problems. A large percentage of job seekers don't effectively communicate the skills they have to do the job, and they answer one or more "problem" questions poorly. Trust us, this is a big problem. If you leave the interview without having answered one or more problem questions well, your odds of getting a job offer are greatly decreased.

While thousands of problem interview questions are possible, we have listed just 10 that, if you can plan how to answer them well, will prepare you for most interviews.

Top 10 Problem Questions

1. Why don't you tell me about yourself?
2. Why should I hire you?
3. What are your major strengths?
4. What are your major weaknesses?
5. What sort of pay do you expect to receive?
6. How does your previous experience relate to the jobs we have here?
7. What are your plans for the future?
8. What will your former employer (or references) say about you?
9. Why are you looking for this type of position, and why here?
10. Why don't you tell me about your personal situation?

We don't have the space here to give thorough answers to all of these questions, and there are potentially hundreds of additional questions you might be asked. Instead, in the next section we suggest several techniques we have developed that you can use to answer almost any interview question.

A Traditional Interview Is Not a Friendly Exchange

It is important to understand what is going on in most interviews. In a traditional interview situation, there is a job opening, and you are one of several (or one of a hundred) applicants. In this setting, the employer's task is to eliminate all but one applicant.

Assuming that you got as far as an interview, the interviewer's questions are designed to elicit information that can be used to screen you out. If you are wise, you know that your task is to avoid getting screened out. It's not an open and honest interaction, is it? This illustrates yet another advantage of nontraditional job search techniques: the ability to talk to an employer before an opening exists. This eliminates the stress of a traditional interview. Employers are not trying to screen you out, and you are not trying to keep them from finding out the bad stuff about you.

The Four-Step Process for Answering Interview Questions

We know this might seem too simple, but the Four-Step Process is easy to remember. Its simplicity allows you to evaluate a question and create a good answer. The technique is based on sound principles and has worked for thousands of people, so consider trying it.

1. **Understand what is really being asked.** Most questions are really designed to find out about your self-management skills and personality. Although they are rarely this blunt, the employer's real questions are often directed at finding out the following:

   - Can I depend on you?

   - Are you easy to get along with? Are you a good worker?

   - Do you have the experience and training to do the job if we hire you?

   - Are you likely to stay on the job for a reasonable period of time and be productive?

     Ultimately, if the employer is not convinced that you will stay and be a good worker, it won't matter if you have the best credentials. He or she won't hire you.

2. **Answer the question briefly, in a non-damaging way.** Acknowledge the facts, but present them as an advantage rather than a disadvantage.

   Many interview questions will encourage you to provide negative information. The classic is the "What are your major weaknesses?" question that we included in our top 10 problem questions list. Obviously, this is a trick question, and many people are not prepared for it. A good response might be to mention something that is not all that damaging, such as "I have been told that I am a perfectionist, sometimes not delegating as effectively as I might." But your answer is not complete until you do the last step.

3. **Answer the real concern by presenting your related skills.** Base your answer on the key skills that you have identified and that are needed in this job. Give examples to support your skills statements. For example, an employer might say to a recent graduate, "We were looking for someone with more experience in this field. Why should we consider you?" Here is one possible answer: "I'm sure there are people who have more experience, but I do have more than six years of work experience, including three years of advanced training and hands-on experience using the latest methods and techniques. Because my training is recent, I am open to new ideas and am used to working hard and learning quickly."

4. **Use a specific example from your experience to support your skills statement.** Many employers believe that your past performance is the best indicator of your future performance. In other words, what you have done in the past lets them know what you will do when faced with similar circumstances in the future. Some employers ask for these specific examples using what are called "behavior-based" interview questions.

   When you hear a question that begins, "Tell me about a time…" or "Give me a specific example…" you will know that you are being asked a behavior-based question. The interviewer wants you to answer the question in three parts: S—Situation (what was going on), A—Actions (what did you do about it), and R—Results (what was the outcome). Once you get the hang of it, these SAR stories are easy to tell and are a great way to convey relevant skills and accomplishments.

   We recommend that you practice some SAR stories and use them whenever possible to bolster your interview answers. The recent graduate quoted above could add to the response given: "For example, in my co-op job I was asked to lead the training for our new product. I had only weeks to learn the product and learn how to teach it. It involved our advanced technology so it was quite challenging. I was able to train our entire 40-person office in another two weeks, and as a result we became the first office in our region to handle a customer installation of the new product."

   As you can see, adding the SAR component to an already good answer will help you to clearly communicate your capabilities in the interview. In the example we presented in Step 2 (about your need to delegate more effectively), a good skills statement might be "I have been working on this problem and have learned to be more willing to let my staff do things, making sure that they have good training and supervision. I've found that their performance improves, and it frees me up to do other things."

   > **Tip:** *Whatever your situation, learn to use it to your advantage. It is essential to communicate your skills during an interview, and the Four-Step Process gives you a technique that can dramatically improve your responses. It works!*

Then, you could add a SAR story to strengthen this good response. "When I took on a high-level project for our chairman, I decided to let go of one of my key responsibilities, preparing end-of-the-month reports for our management team. I trained my staff and closely supervised the first time they handled this, and they performed just great. Since then, I've had to spend only about 15 minutes a month reviewing their work, instead of the 6 hours I used to spend creating the reports. Morale has really gone up in the office, and I've kept every deadline for my new, very challenging project."

Step 7: Follow Up on All Contacts

People who follow up with potential employers and with others in their network get jobs faster than those who do not. This is another principle that seems too simple to be so important, but it is true.

As we discussed in chapter 4, we recommend that you send a thank-you note to every person who helps you in your job search, and that you do so immediately—within 24 hours of speaking with that person.

It is important that you develop a system to keep track of who helped you, when you contacted them, and what you need to do next to stay in touch and keep them aware of your progress.

Use a simple 3 × 5–inch card to keep essential information about each person in your network. Buy a 3 × 5–inch card file box and tabs for each day of the month. File the cards under the date you want to contact the person, and the rest is easy. We have found that staying in touch with a good contact every other week can pay off big.

Tip: *You can take advantage of technology to help you manage your job search. A contact-management program such as ACT! enables you to create electronic "cards" for each contact and integrate them into your weekly schedule. You might also create a spreadsheet with a program such as Microsoft Excel where you log your activity and keep details on each person and organization. You could also use a PDA such as a Palm Pilot to keep track of your appointments and contacts.*

Here's a sample card to give you ideas for creating your own if you use the index-card method.

```
ORGANIZATION:    Mutual Health Insurance
CONTACT PERSON:  Anna Tomey              PHONE: 317-355-0216
SOURCE OF LEAD:  Aunt Ruth
NOTES.  1/10 Called. Anna on vacation. Call back 4/15. 4/15 Interview set
        4/20 at 1:30. 4/20 Anna showed me around. They use the same computers
        we used in school! (Friendly people.) Sent thank-you note and JIST
        Card, call back 5/1. 5/1 Second interview 5/8 at 9 a.m.!
```

Figure 6-2: Sample job lead card.

Key Points: Chapter 6

Here are the key points of this chapter:

- Approach your job search as if it were a job itself.

- Get organized and spend at least 25 hours per week actively looking.

- Know your skills and have a clear job objective.

- Get lots of interviews, including exploratory interviews.

- Have a good answer to the question "Why should I hire you?"

- Follow up on all the leads you generate and send out lots of thank-you notes and JIST Cards.

- Pay attention to all the details; then be yourself in the interview. Remember that employers are people, too. They will hire someone who they feel will do the job well, be reliable, and fit easily into the work environment.

- Tell the employer that you want the job and why.

- Believe in yourself and ask people to help you. They will!

Index

© JIST Works